Workbook

BACKPACK 1

Second Edition

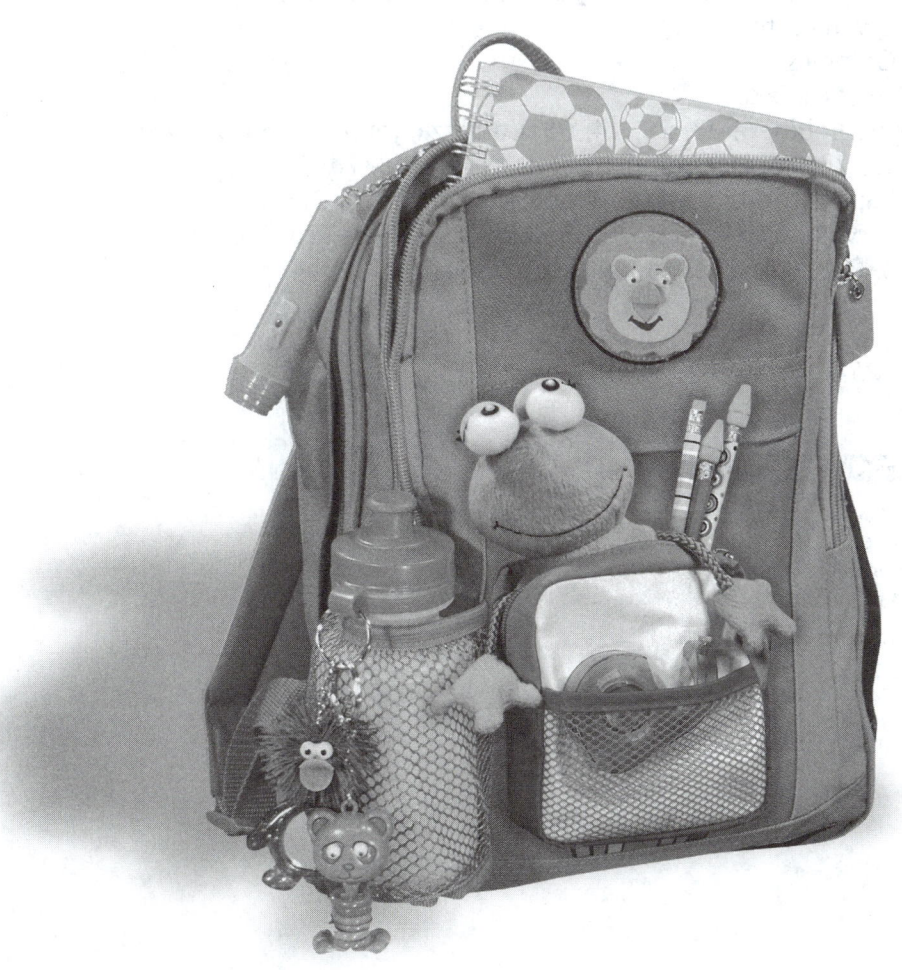

Mario Herrera · Diane Pinkley

PEARSON
Longman

Backpack 1, Second Edition
Workbook

Pearson Education, 10 Bank Street, White Plains, NY 10606, USA

Staff credits: The people who made up the *Backpack 1* Workbook team, representing editorial, production, design, and manufacturing, are Rhea Banker, Carol Brown, Sarah Bupp, Iris Candelaria, Tracey Cataldo, Gina DiLillo, Christine Edmonds, Ed Lamprich, Maria Pia Marrella, Linda Moser, Diane Pinkley, Edie Pullman, Susan Saslow, and Andrew Vaccaro.
Text composition: TSI Graphics
Text font: 16 pt HSP Helvetica Text
Illustration credits: Boyer, Robin, 6, 23, 28, 44, 65; Carrozza, John, 15, 54, 77, 78; Fry, Collin, 13, 35, 51, 63, 73, 76; Linstromberg, Ruth, 1, 24, 38, 74, 75; McClurkan, Rob, 45; Miranda, Hugo, 91–106; Monroy, Manuel, 26, 27; Montiel, Javier, 21; Nethery, Susan, 43, 64, 71, 88; Radtke, Becky, 4, 18, 25, 34, 53, 61, 83; Silver-Thompson, Pattie, 5, 6, 23, 33, 41; Tobin, Nancy, 7, 8; Yoshikwa, Sachiko, 11

ISBN-13: 978-0-13-245125-3
ISBN-10: 0-13-245125-5

PEARSON LONGMAN ON THE **WEB**

Pearsonlongman.com offers online resources for teachers and students. Access our Companion Websites, our online catalog, and our local offices around the world.

Visit us at **pearsonlongman.com**.

11 2019

Printed in the United States of America

Contents

Ready for School

 **1** **Listen and color. Cut and glue.**

Hello!

Hello! I'm Ricky Red.
Look! I have one pen and
   I'm ready for school.

Hello. I'm Gracie Green.
Look! I have two books and
   I'm ready for school.

Hello. I'm Bobby Blue.
Look! I have three erasers and
   I'm ready for school.

Hello! Do you hear the bell ring?
   It's time for school and we're ready to go!

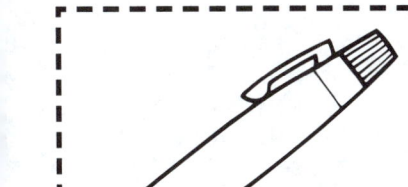

2 Draw and color. Write.

What's your name?

My name is

_____.

TRACK 4

3 Count and write. Listen and check.

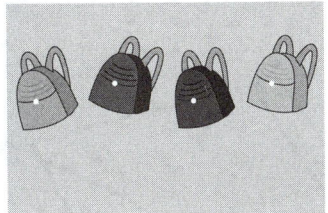

1. ____4____ backpacks

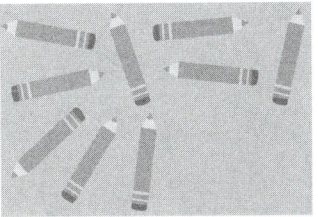

2. _____ pencils

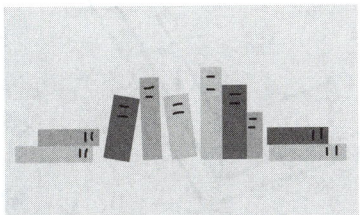

3. _____ books

4. _____ crayons

5. _____ erasers

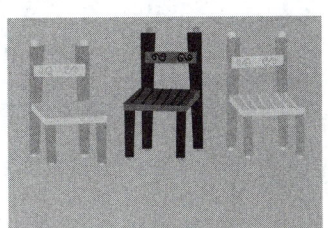

6. _____ chairs

Unit 1

3

TRACK 5

4 Color. Listen and point. Write.

1 = blue 2 = green
3 = red

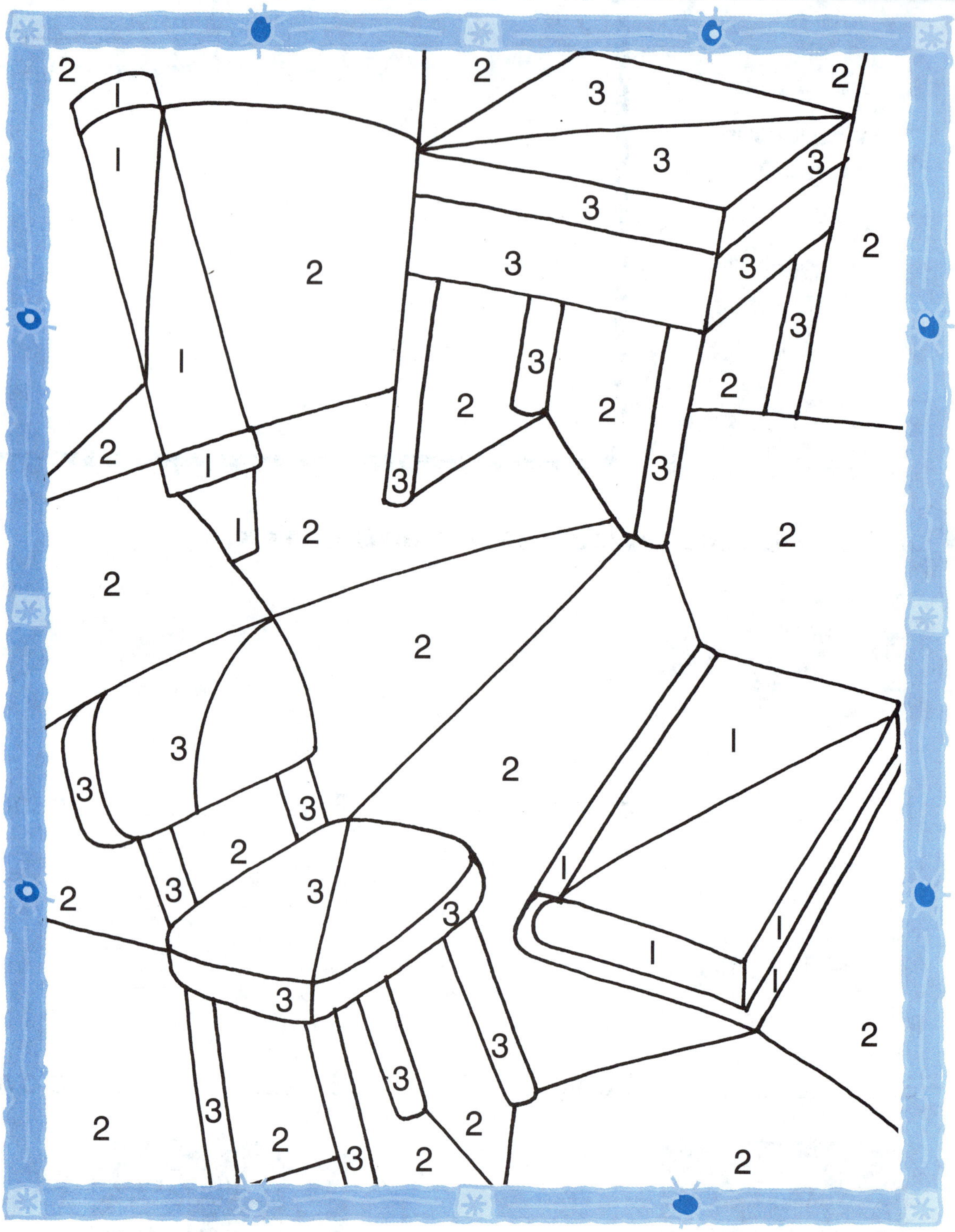

b ______________________

ch ______________________

t ______________________

cr ______________________

5 **Listen and match. Draw a line. Color. Write.**

Hey, Jill!

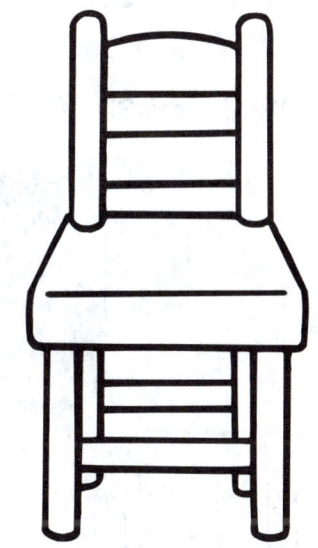

Hey, Jill!
What's this?
It's a pen, Bill.

_____

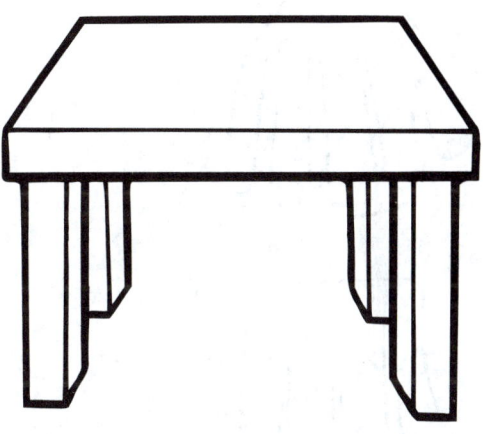

Hey, Ken!
What's this?
It's a chair, Jen.

_____

Hey, Matt!
What's this?
It's a table, Pat.

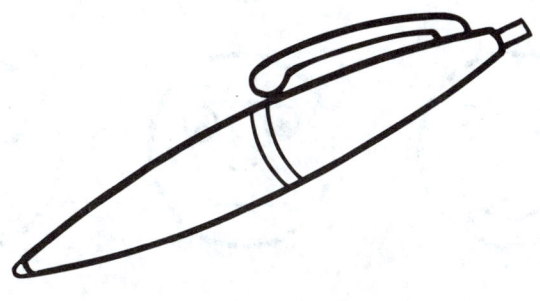

_____

Guess Again

6 **Read *Guess Again*. Match. Draw a line.**

What's this?

It's a desk.

7 **Do you like the story? Draw a face.**

8 **Draw your classroom. Color and say.**

Review

1

2

3

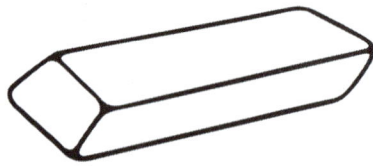

4

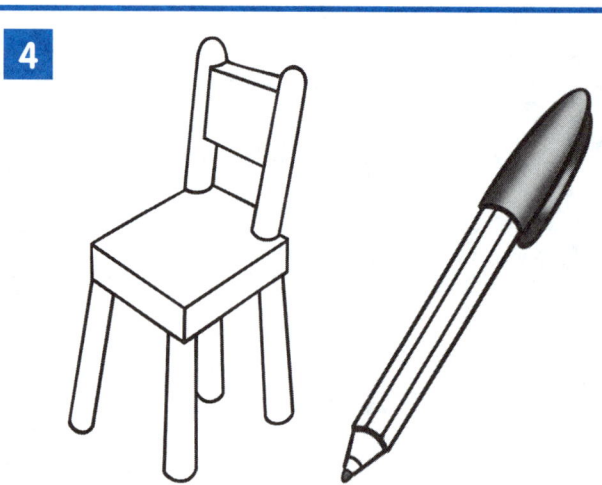

5

6

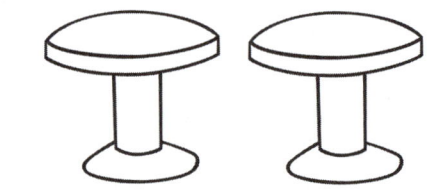

Cut-out Activity ✂ - - - - - - - - - - - - - - -

A. Find a partner.
B. Cut. Match and say.

Partners lay both sets of cards facedown. They take turns turning over two cards at a time.
If the two cards match, the student keeps the pair. If not, the two cards are placed facedown
again. When students find a match, they name the number and show that number of fingers.

People We Love

 **1** Listen. Cut and glue in order.

My Family Song

1	2	3

4	5

② Match. Draw a line.

my father

my mother

my sister

me

my brother

my sister

the baby

③ Listen. Write the number.

1. She is my sister.

2. He is my father.

3. He is my brother.

4. She is my mother.

4 Listen and match. Draw a line and say.

1. | Who am I? |

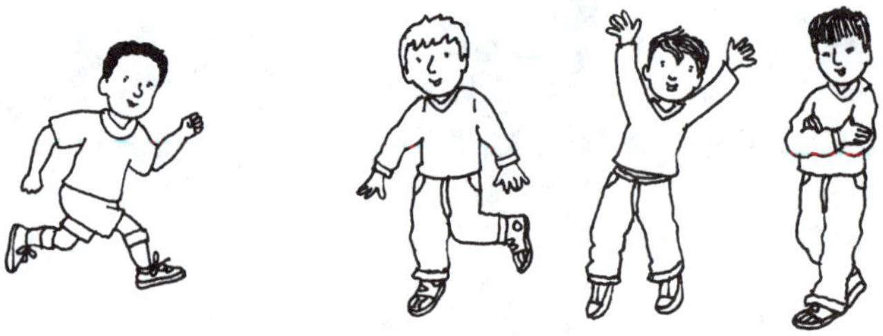

2. | Who am I? |

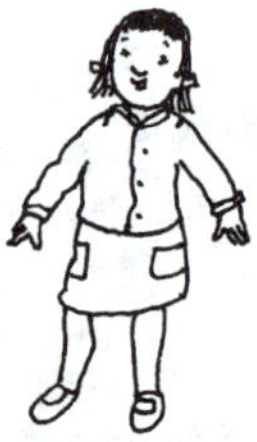

3. | Who am I? |

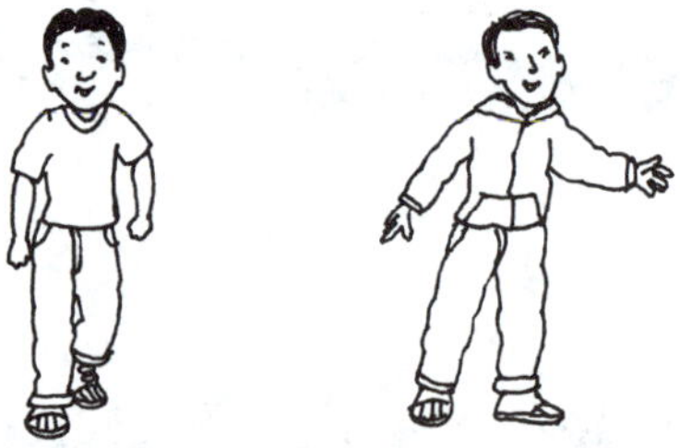

4. | Who am I? |

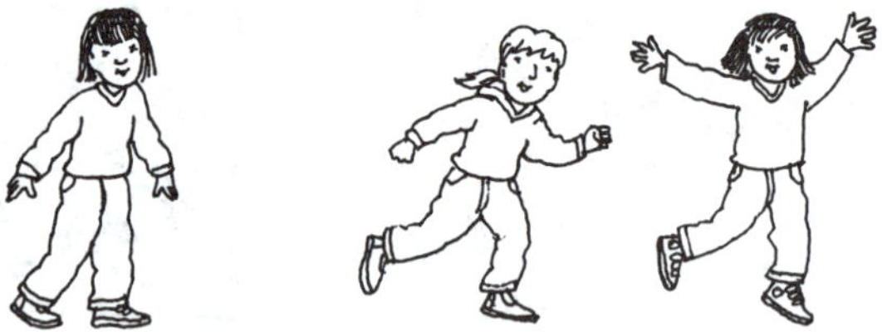

5 Draw two brothers and two sisters.

 **6** **Listen. Write.**

TRACK 11

Clap for Your Family

Sisters, sisters.
How many sisters
do you have?

_____

Brothers, brothers.
How many brothers
do you have?

_____

Let's Play

7 Read *Let's Play*. Match. Draw lines.

8 Do you like the story? Draw a face.

   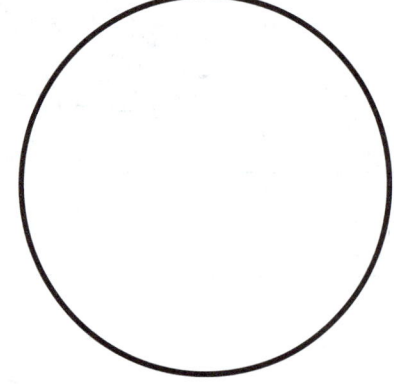

Who's on your team? Draw and say.

Review

 TRACK 12 **10** **Listen. Circle *yes* or *no*.**

1.

yes   no

2.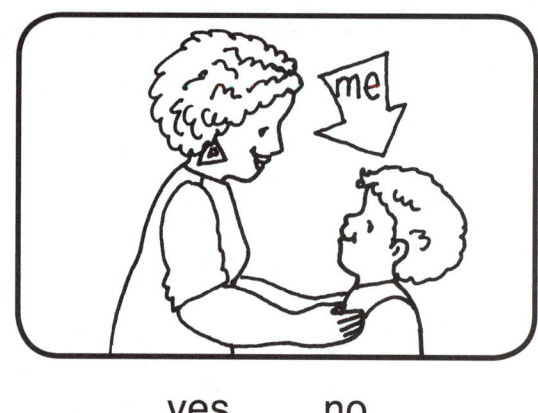

yes   no

3.

yes   no

4.

yes   no

5.

yes   no

6.

yes   no

Cut-out Activity ✂ - - - - - - - - - - - - - - - - -

A. Find a partner.
B. Cut. Make words and say.

t	p	r
e	o	s
m	a	c
i	f	b

Students combine the alphabet cards to form words. (Students can use one set or combine
two sets.) Words will vary, but may include the following: *backpack, book, chair, crayon,
desk, eraser, marker, paper, pencil, table, baby, brother, father, mother, sister, yes, no, is,
play, this, one, red,* and *family.*

d	o	i
e	l	n
s	h	a
r	k	y

3 Head to Toes

1 Listen and color. Cut and glue.

Look at Me!

Look at me! I'm in the ocean!
What do you see?
Two arms in the shape of a *V*.
Two arms in the shape of a *V*.

Look at me! I'm in the chair!
What do you see?
A big blue towel and long brown hair.
A big blue towel and long brown hair.

Look at me! I'm in the sand!
What do you see?
A white hat and just one hand.
A white hat and just one hand.

Look at me!

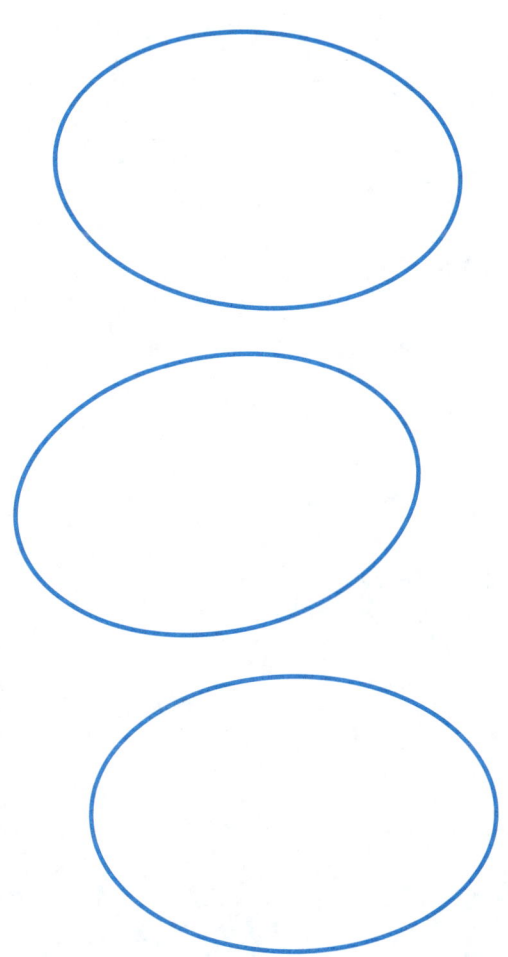

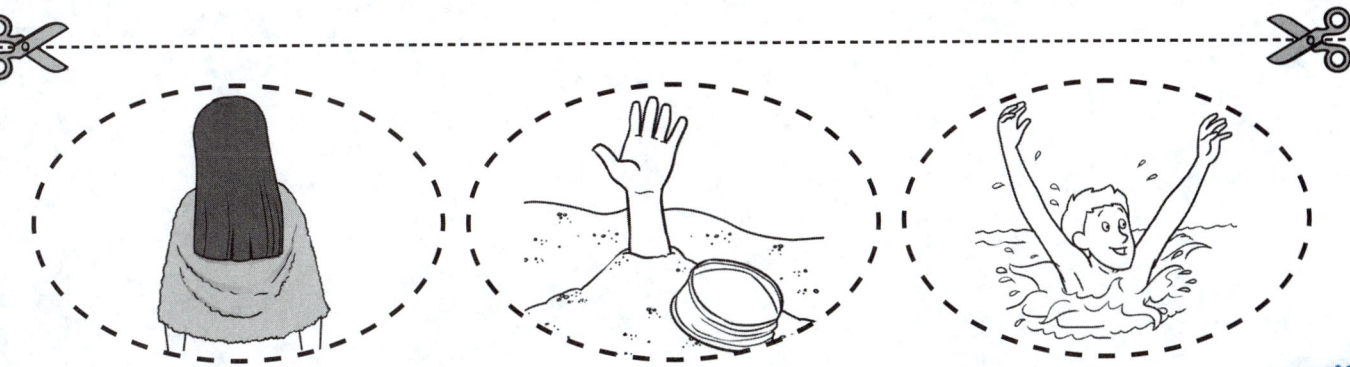

② Match. Draw a line.

It is short.

It is long.

She is little.

He is little.

She is big.

He is big.

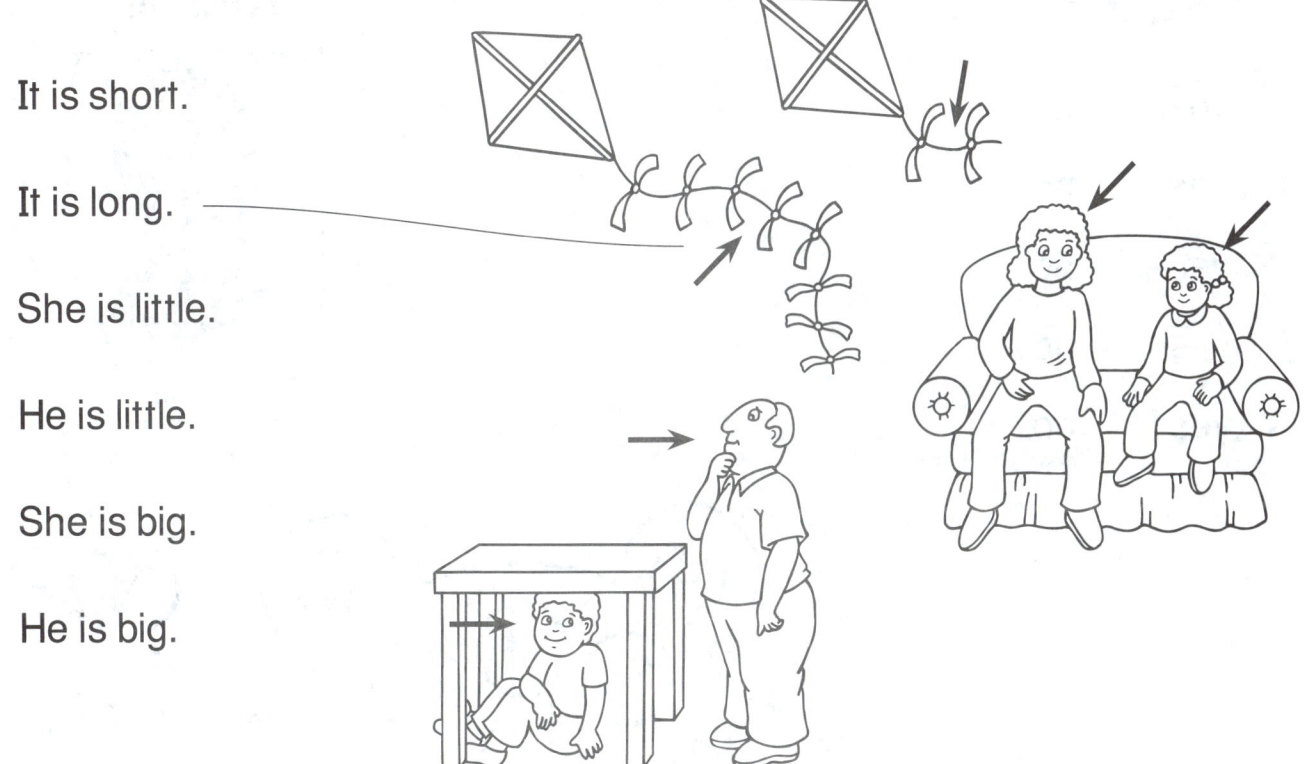

③ Listen and color.

short

long

little

big

4 Listen and count. Circle *yes* or *no*. Color. Say.

1. (yes)   no

2. yes   no

3. yes   no

4. yes   no

5. yes   no

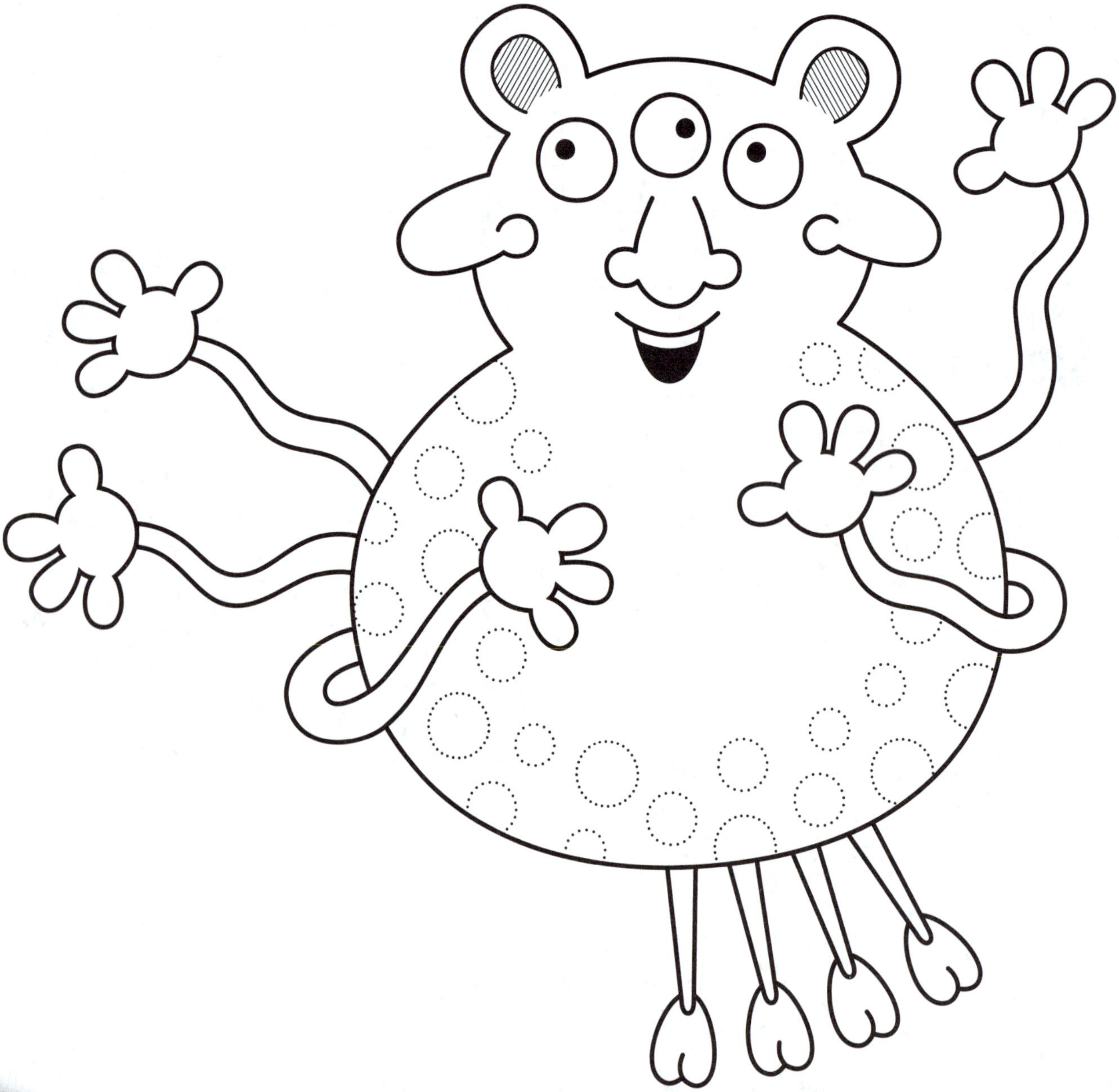

It has three eyes. Yes or no?

TRACK 16

5 **Listen and circle. Draw. Write about you.**

The Spider

1. 2   4   8   eyes.

2. 4   6   8   legs.

3. 1   2   3   head.

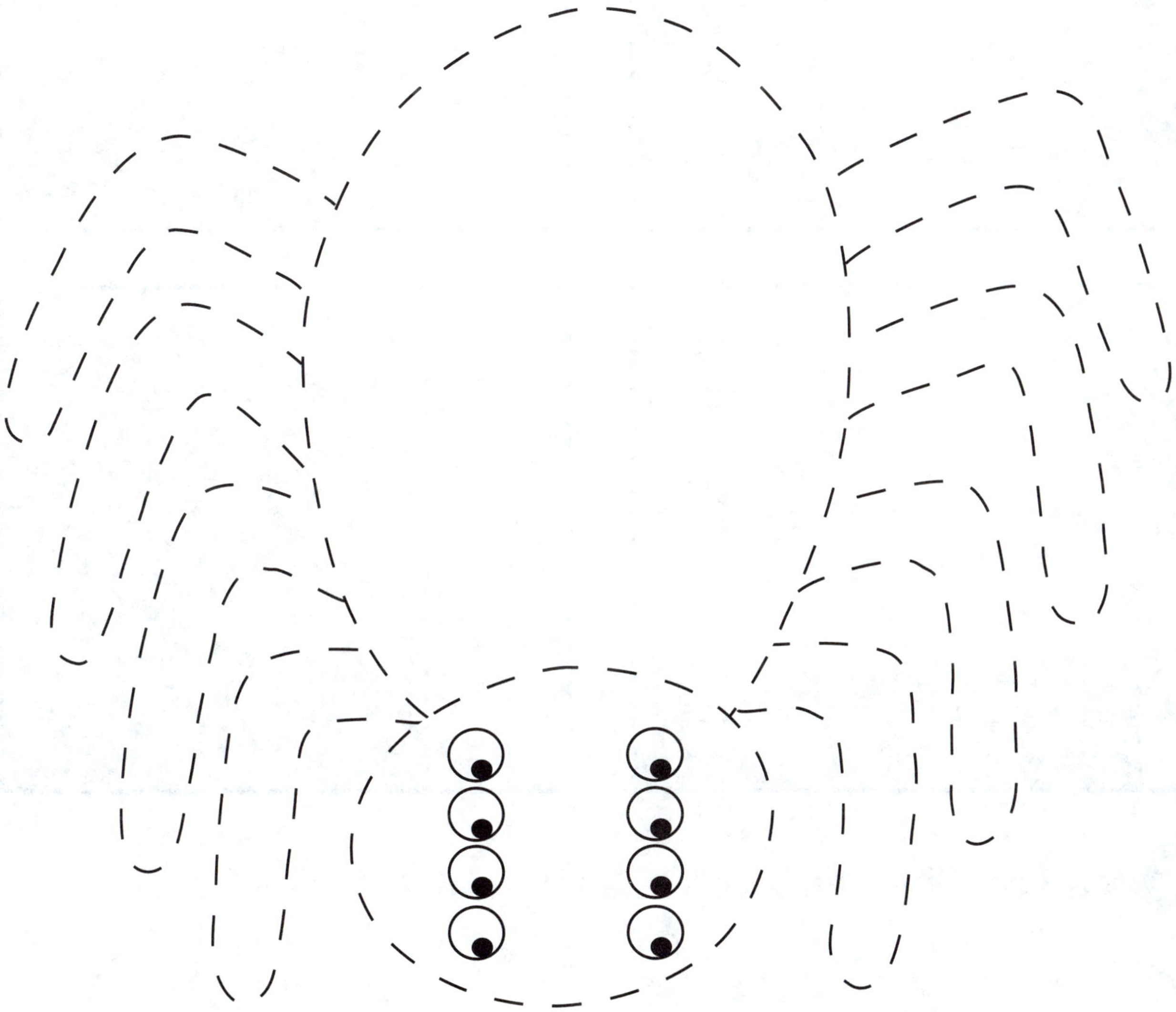

My name is _____. I have _____ eyes.

I have _____ legs. I have _____ head.

Unit 3

25

What Is It?

6 Read *What Is It?* Look. Write the number.

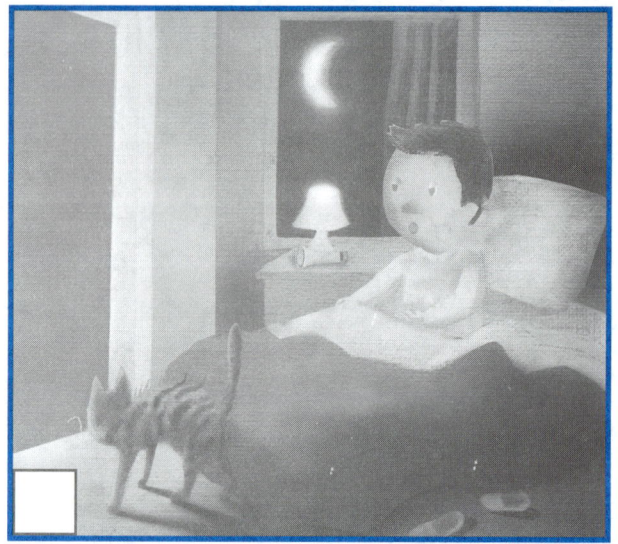

7 Do you like the story? Draw a face.

Look and write.

cat   monster   mother

It's a _____.

It's Mark's _____.

It's not a _____!

Review

 **TRACK 17**

9 **Listen and circle. Color.**

1.

2.

3.

4.

Cut-out Activity ✂

Draw what you know. Show and say.

Ready for School	People We Love	Head to Toes

Students draw four vocabulary items from Units 1, 2, and 3. They show their drawings in groups and name each item they drew. Encourage the other group members to comment on the drawings. (*Nice job. Good work.*)

Things I Wear

1 **Listen and color. Cut and glue.**

I Want Shoes

I'm wearing a jacket, a , and pants,
   a shirt and pants.
I need one thing so I can dance.
So I can dance.

My  is blue, and my shirt is new.
My shirt is new.
My clothes are blue.
Now I want some shoes.

I'm wearing a jacket, a shirt, and .
I want some shoes so I can dance,
      so I can dance,
      so I can dance.

 -

Unit 4
31

2 Listen. Color the spaces. Write.

P = pink   B = black   W = white

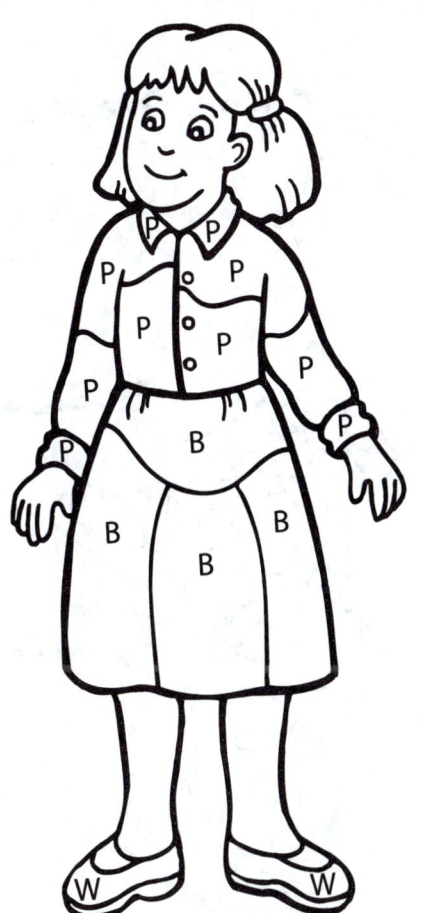

1. She's wearing a _____ shirt.

2. She's wearing a _____ skirt.

3. She's wearing _____ shoes.

3 Read. Draw and color.

pink socks   a blue table   a black crayon

a red hat   orange pants   a green book

Color. Draw a line from _Start_ to _End_. Say.

1 = blue	2 = red	3 = green	4 = yellow	5 = orange

34

5 **Listen and circle. Unscramble and write. Draw.**

What's This?

1. That's my new _____.   hat   jacket   pants

2. That's my blue _____.   shirt   dress   sweater

3. It's a pair of _____.   socks   gloves   sneakers

(t a e c j k)   (w a s r e t e)   (k s o c s)

_____   _____   _____

The Fun House

6 Read *The Fun House.* Write. Match and draw lines.

| blouse | gloves | hat | shirt | shoes |

1. small _____

2. a big _____

3. a funny _____

7 Do you like the story? Draw a face.

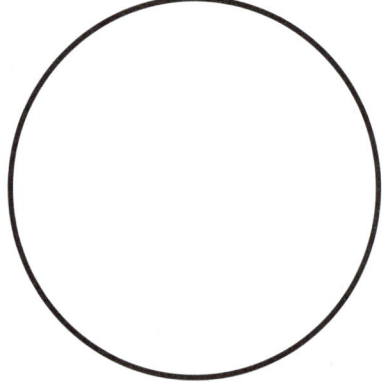

8 **Draw yourself in the Fun House.**
Color and say.

Review

TRACK 21

9 **Listen and color.**

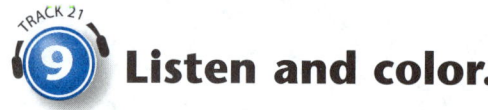

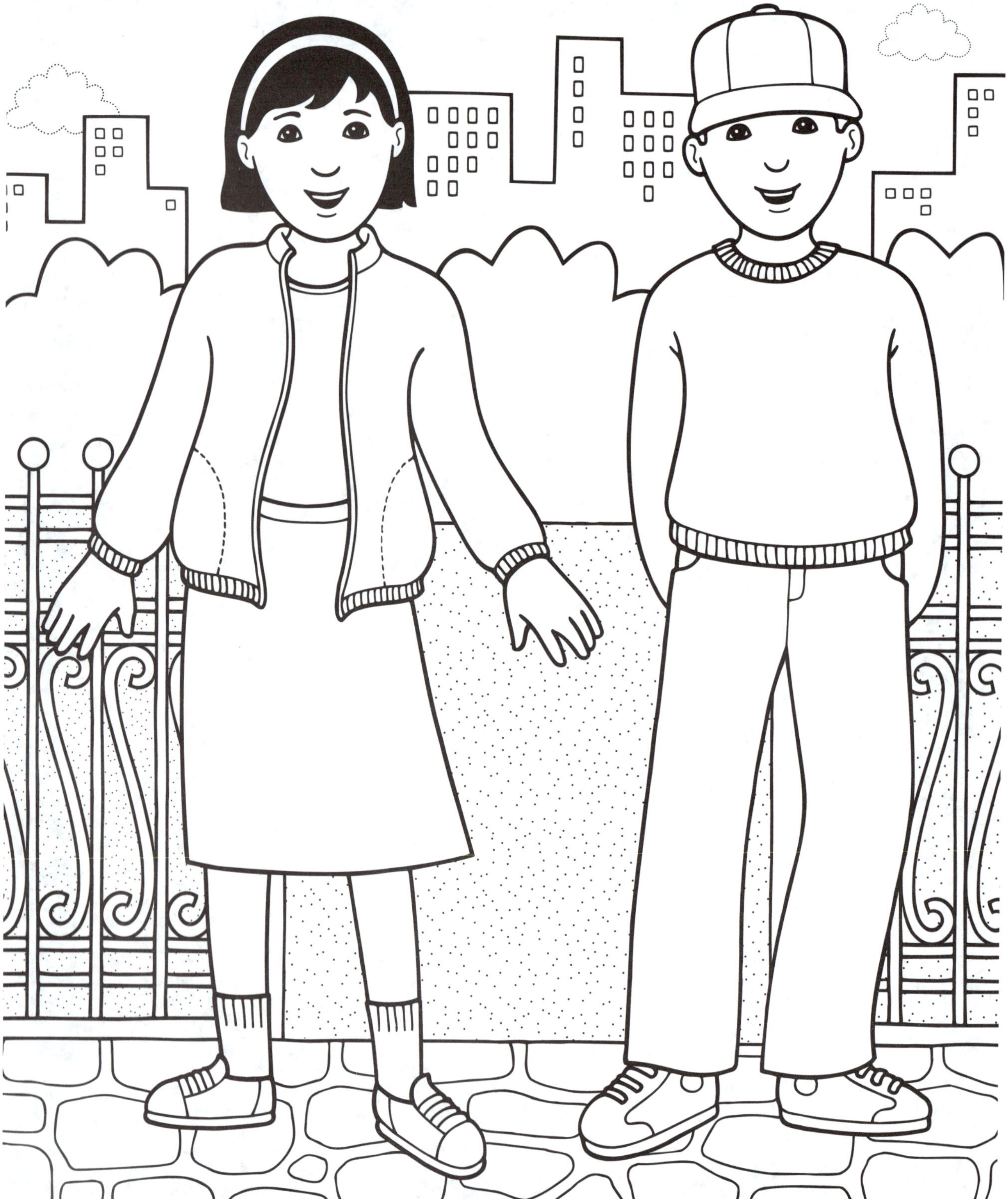

Cut-out Activity

A. Find a partner. Take turns.
B. What is she wearing? Say.
   Listen and draw.

Student A tells Student B to draw a boy and his clothing according to instructions. (*Draw a shirt. Draw a jacket.*) Student B follows the instructions. Then Student B tells Student A to draw a girl and her clothing according to instructions.

Cut-out Activity ✂--------------------------------

A. **Find a partner. Take turns.**
B. **What is he wearing? Say.**
   Listen and draw.

5 At Home

TRACK 22

1 **Listen and color. Cut and glue.**

Let's Make a House!

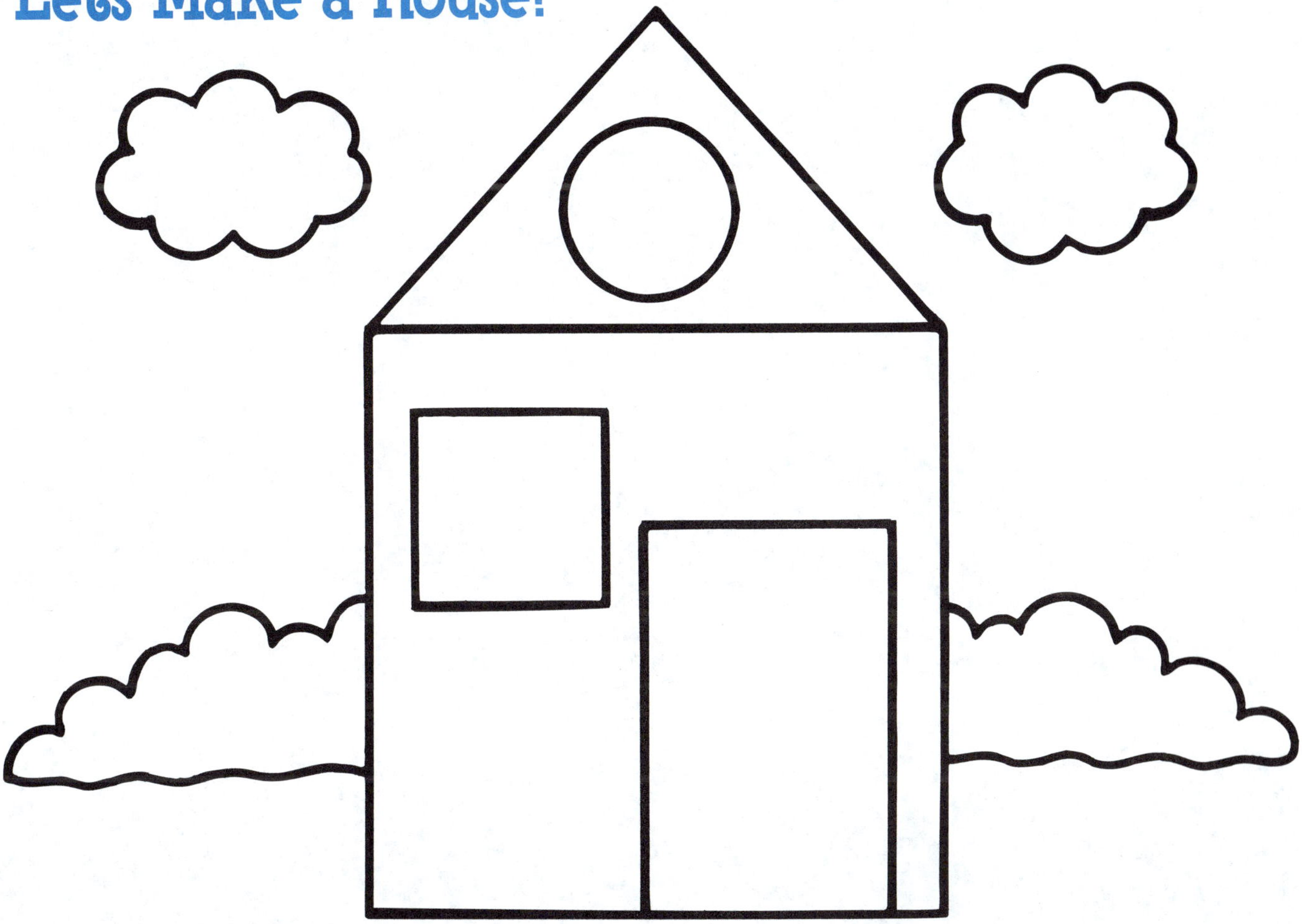

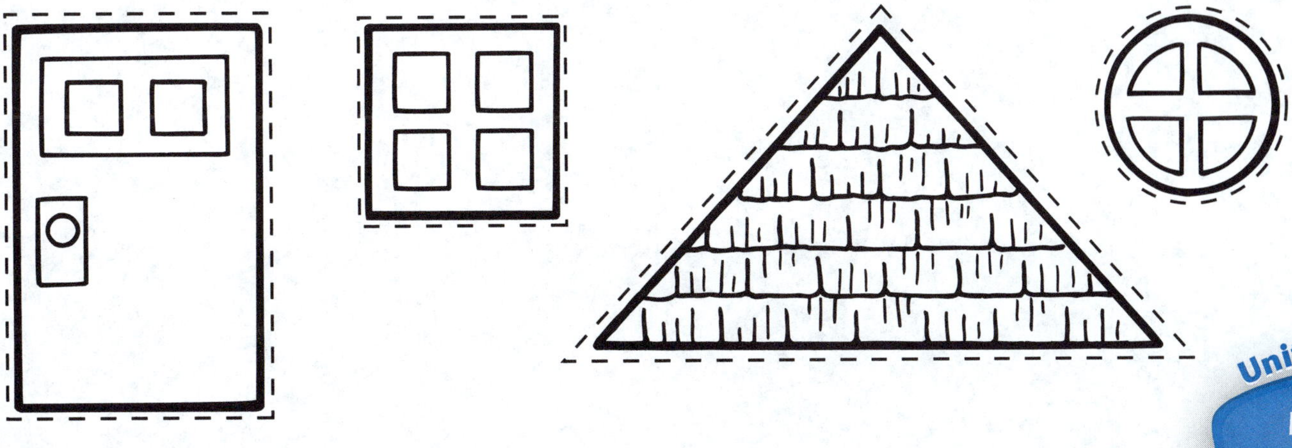

2 Match. Draw a line and say.

triangle

rectangle

square

circle

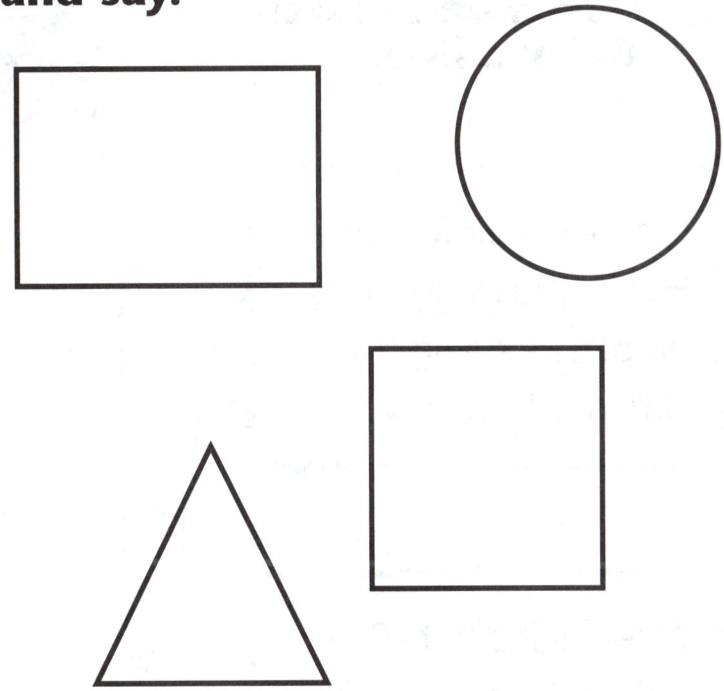

3 Color and count. Write the number word. Listen and check.

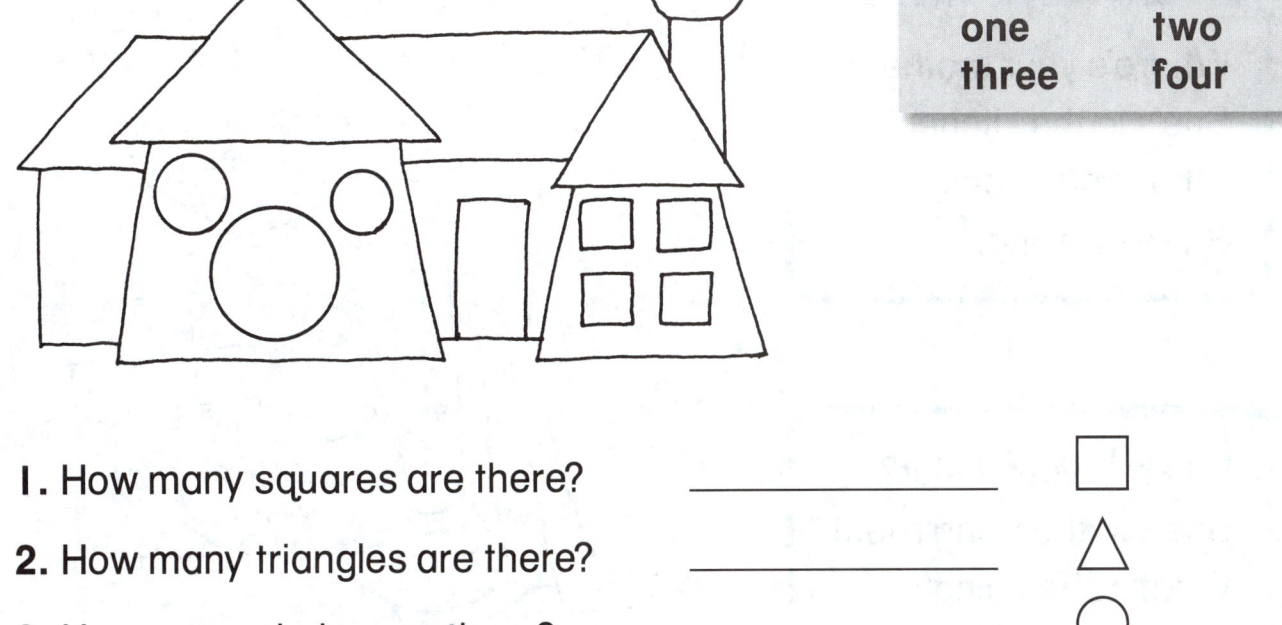

| one | two |
| three | four |

1. How many squares are there?   _____ ☐

2. How many triangles are there?   _____ △

3. How many circles are there?   _____ ○

4. How many rectangles are there?   _____ ▭

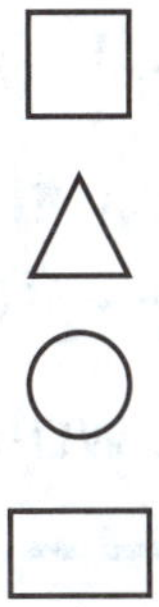

4 **Listen and match. Draw a line.**

Where's your father?
He's in the living room.
What's he doing?
He's reading.

Where's the baby?
He's in the bathroom.
What's he doing?
He's taking a bath.

Where's your mother?
She's in the kitchen.
What's she doing?
She's cooking.

Where's your sister?
She's in the living room.
What's she doing?
She's watching TV.

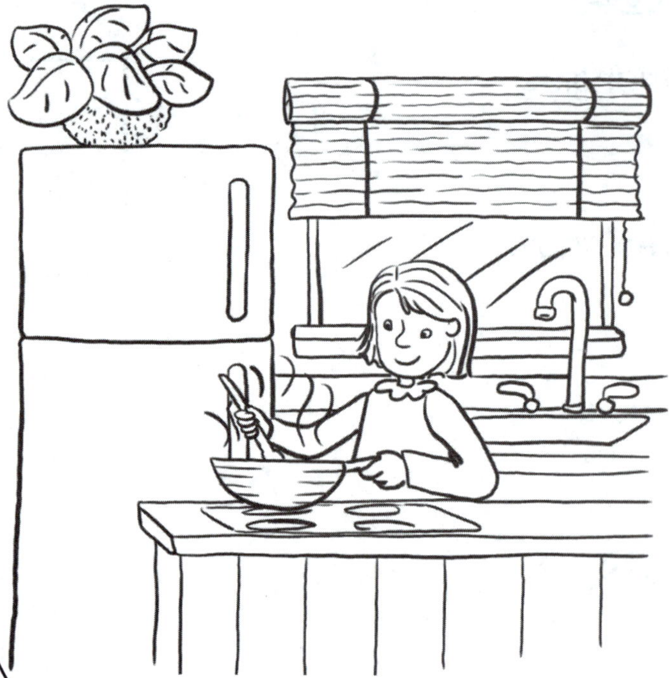

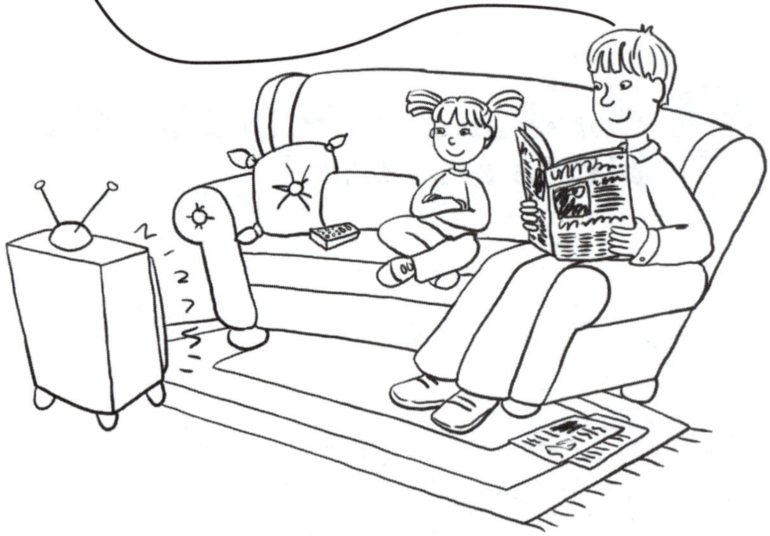

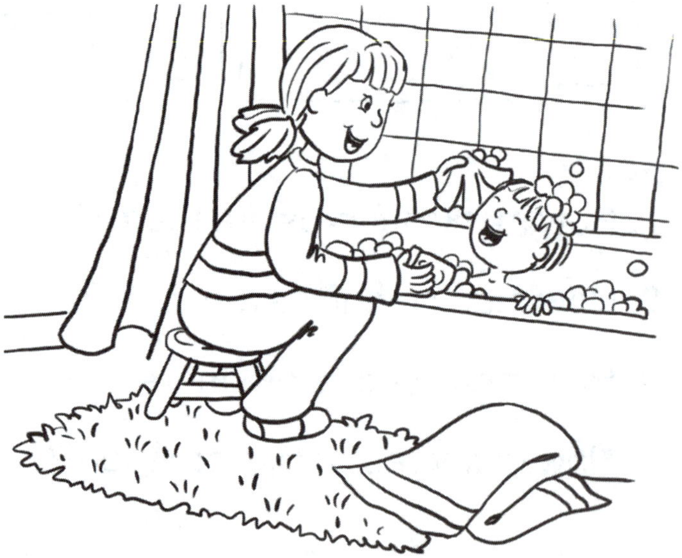

5 Listen and draw a line. Say.

We Are Busy

She
is

He
is

We
are

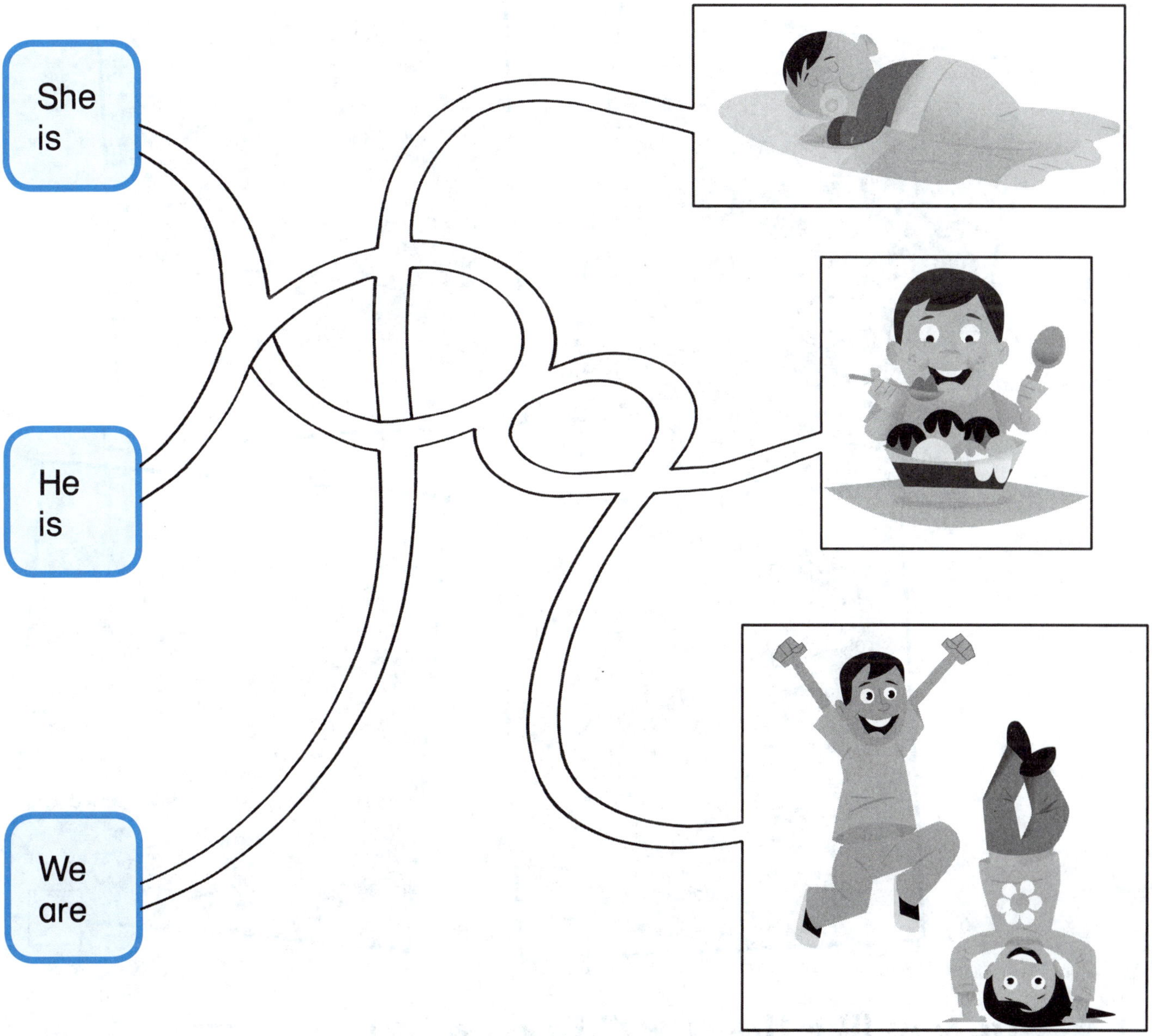

6 What are you doing? Write.

| coloring | cutting | reading | writing |

I'm _____.

Home with Mom

7 Read *Home with Mom*. What happens?
Look. Write the numbers.

1

8 Do you like the story? Draw a face.

   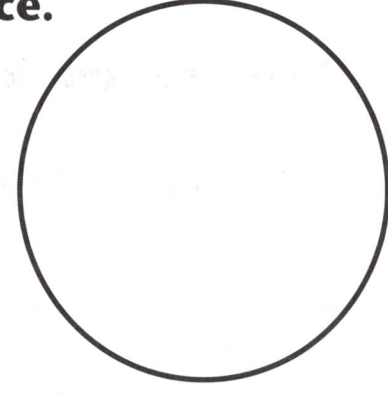

9 **Draw your favorite room.**
Color. Write.

My _____

Review

 **10** **Listen and match. Draw a line.**

1. father

2. mother

3. brother

4. sister

5. baby

11 **Draw a room with grandparents.**
Where are they? Say.

Cut-out Activity ✂ -

A. Find a partner.
B. Cut. Make words and say.

a	n	t
e	m	s
d	i	k
v	b	o

Students combine the alphabet cards to form words. (Students can use one set or combine
two sets.) Words will vary, but may include the following: *bathroom, bedroom, kitchen,
living room, green, red, blue, book, chair, glue, pen, pencil, one, three, seven, ten, mother,
sister, arm, ear, hand, head, mouth, nose, shirt, skirt, socks, gloves,* and *hat.*

Unit 5

49

l	g	h
u	s	p
h	r	i
e	a	c

6 On the Farm

TRACK 27

1 Listen and color. Cut and glue.

All Around the Farm

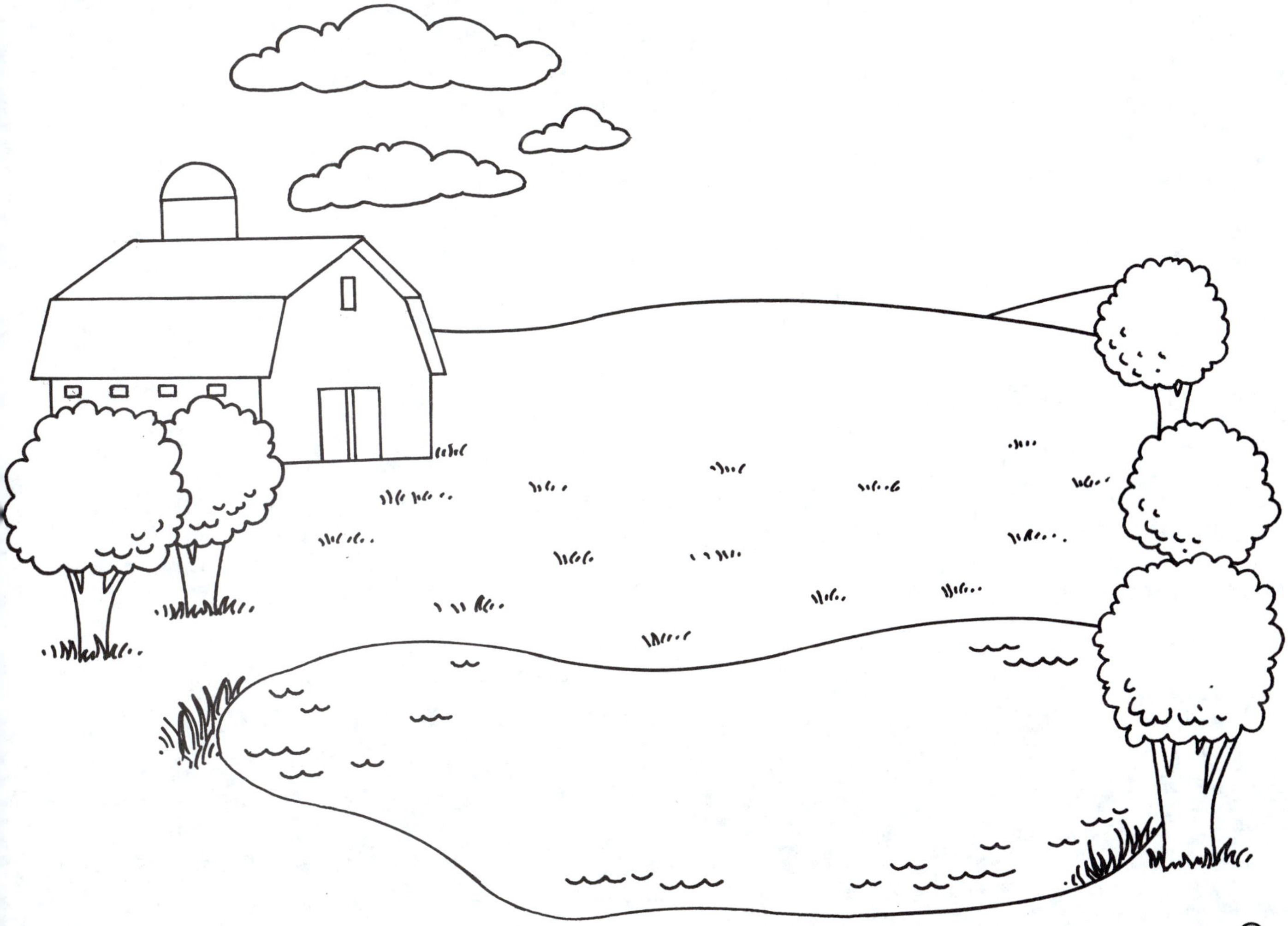

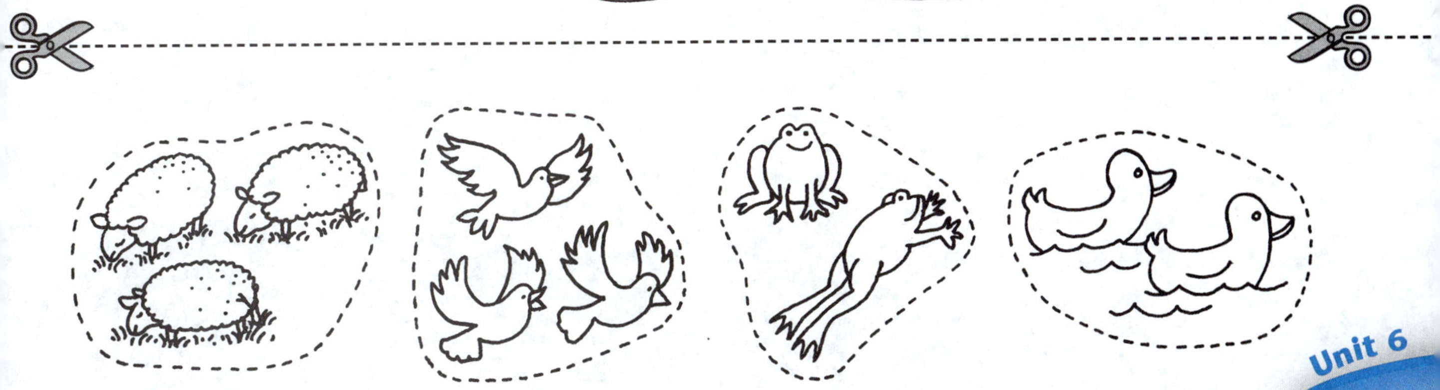

Read and color. Match and draw a line.

a big orange cat

a little white cat

a big blue fish

a little pink fish

a big black and white cow

a little brown cow

TRACK 28
 **Listen and match. Draw a line.**

1. This is a bird.
   It's a little bird.

2. This is a cat.
   It's a big cat.

3. This is a frog.
   It's a big frog.

4 Listen and write. Match. Draw a line.

| climbing | flying | running | swimming | walking |

1. The farmer is

_____.

2. The farmer is

_____.

3. The farmer is

_____.

4. The farmer is

_____.

5. The farmer is

_____.

5 **Listen. Circle the word. Write.**

Look and See!

This is fun.
Look and see!
The birds are _____.   **walking   dancing**
They're dancing with me.

This is fun.
Look and see!
The birds are _____.   **running   flying**
They're flying with me!

6 **Draw and color.**

The birds are dancing.   The birds are flying.

Out of My House!

7 Read *Out of My House!* Circle the animals from the story. What are they doing? Say.

1.
 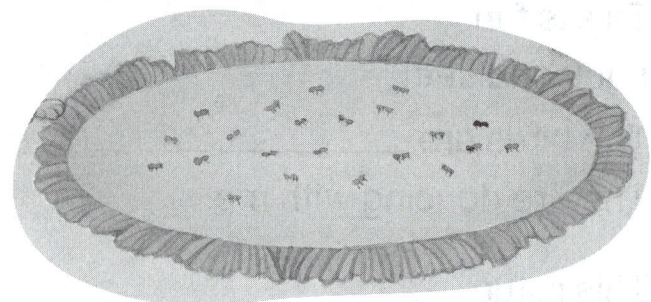

2.

3.

8 Do you like the story? Draw a face.

   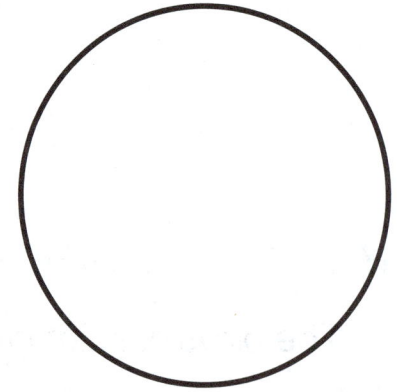

Draw three animals in the house. Color and say.

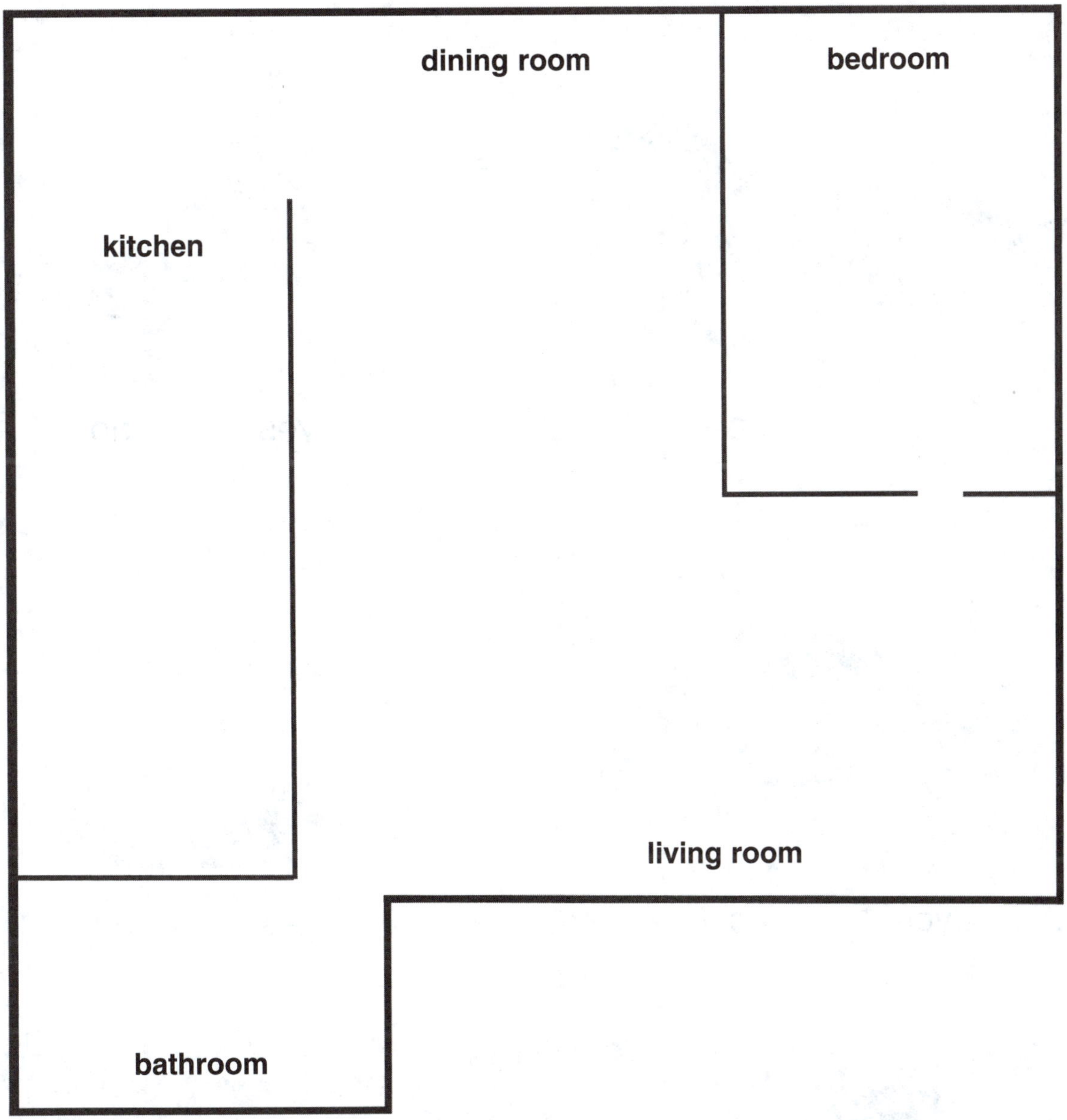

dining room

bedroom

kitchen

living room

bathroom

Review

10 **Listen. Circle _yes_ or _no_.**

1.

    yes   no

2.

    yes   no

3.

    yes   no

4.

    yes   no

5.

    yes   no

6.

    yes   no

Cut-out Activity

Draw and write. Show and say.

◯ = animal

▢ = room

△ = clothes

Students draw and color an item of clothing on one side of the triangle and write what it is on the other side of the triangle. They draw and label an animal in the circle, and a room of a house in the square. Pairs of students make a mobile using the finished shapes.

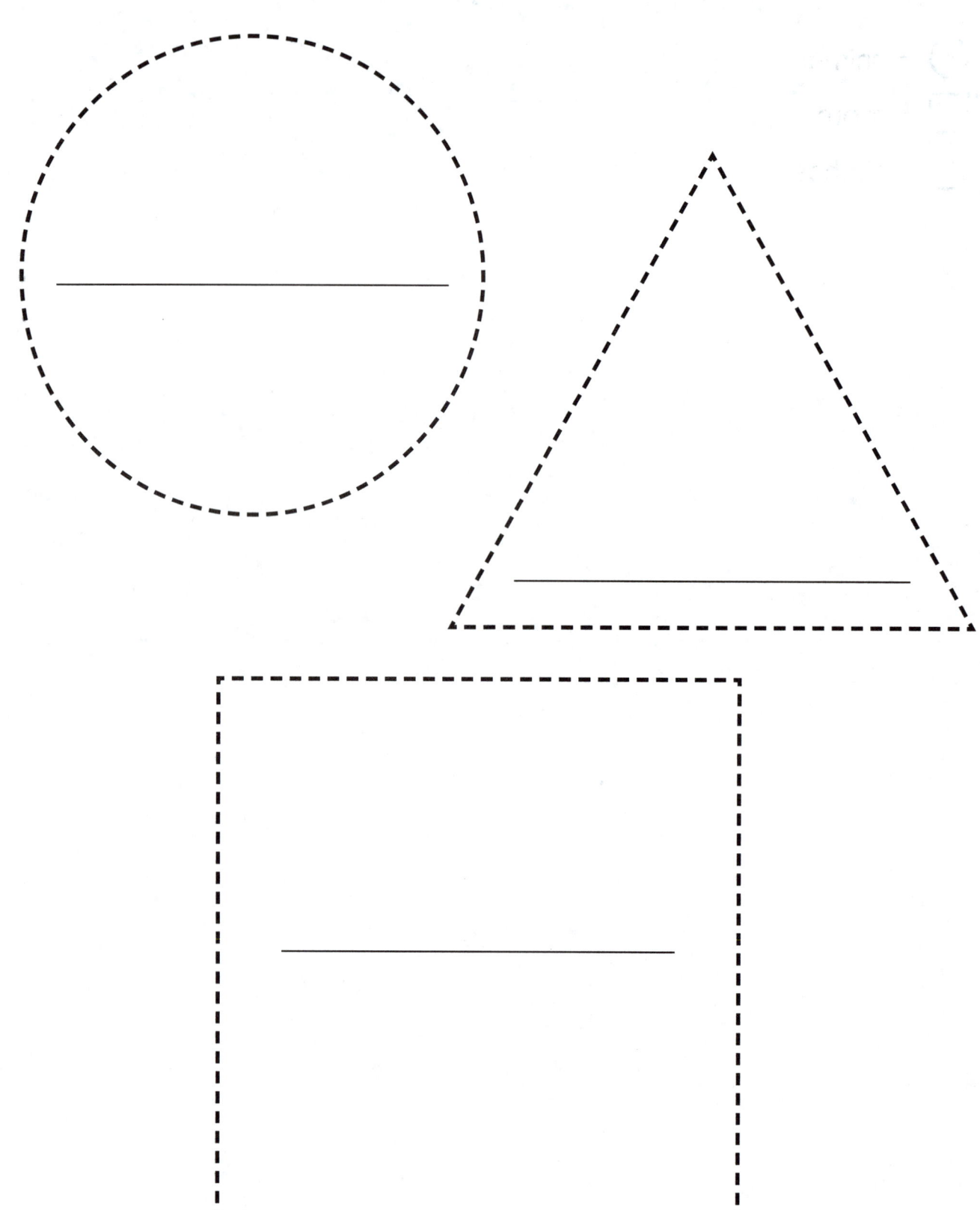

7 Celebrations

TRACK 32

1 Listen. Cut and glue.

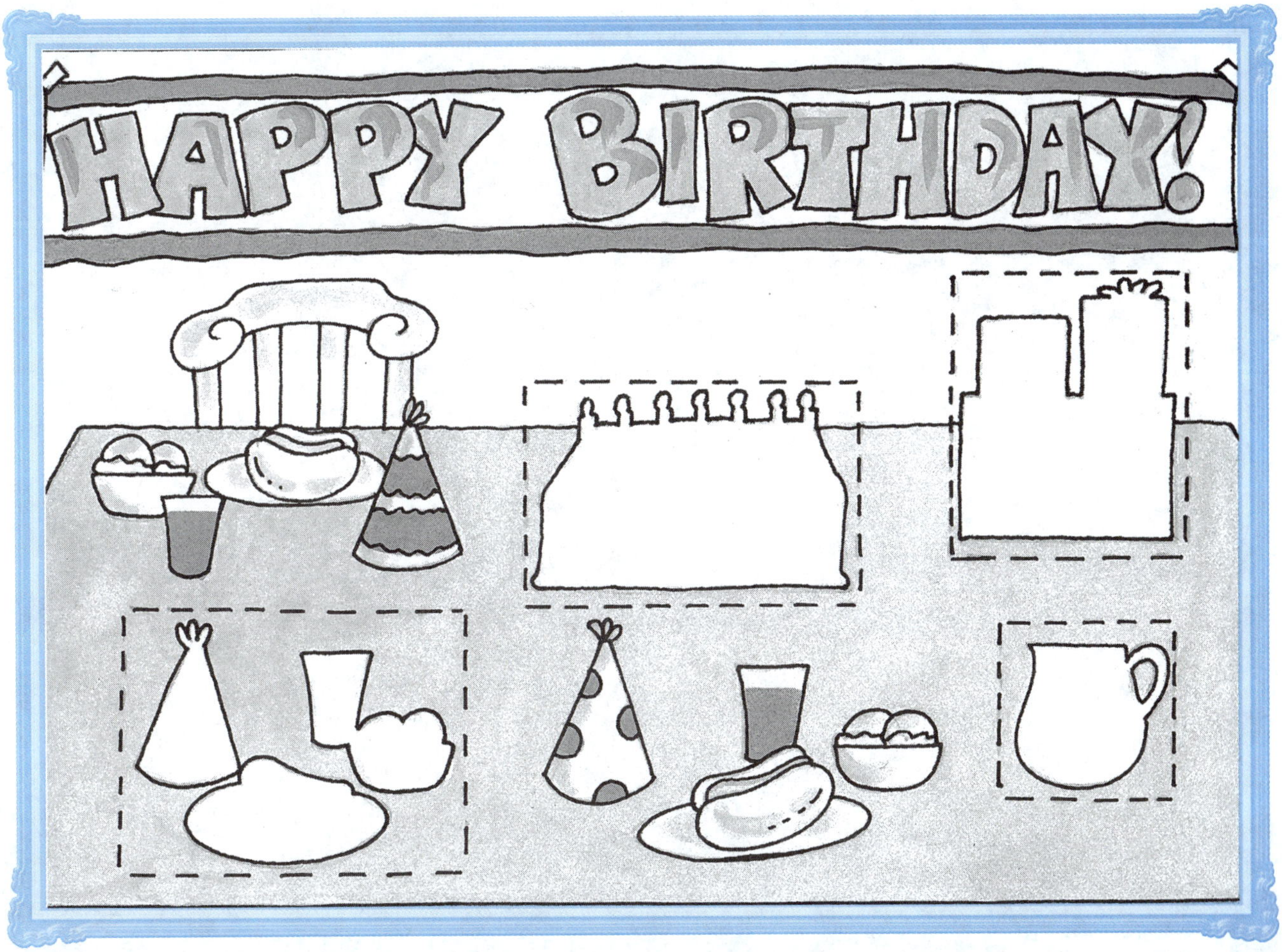
HAPPY BIRTHDAY!

Happy
Birthday

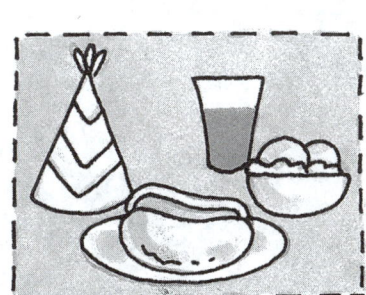

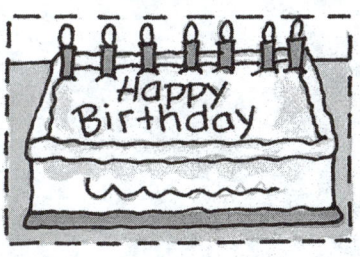

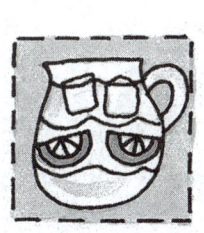

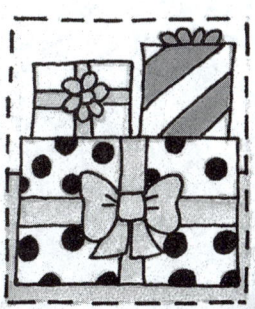

Match. Draw a line. Color.

I'm six years old.

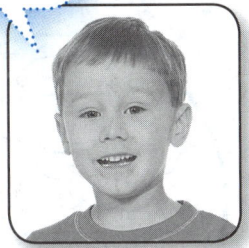
I'm seven years old.

I'm eight years old.

 **Listen and write.**

| Sunday | Monday | Tuesday | Wednesday |
| Thursday | Friday | Saturday | |

1. My birthday is on _____ this year.

2. My father's birthday is on _____ this year.

3. My mother's birthday is on _____ this year.

4. My sister's birthday is on _____ this year.

 TRACK 34

4 Listen. Circle *yes* or *no*.

1. yes   no

2. yes   no

3. yes   no

4. yes   no

5. yes   no

6. yes   no

5 Write and draw.

What do you have?

I have _____.

 TRACK 35

6 Listen and match. Draw a line.

A Celebration

Today I have a present.
It's little, blue, and round.
It's for a celebration,
    and it makes a funny sound!

Today I have a present
    in a box that's green and square.
It's for a celebration.
It's something I can wear!

Today I have a present.
Whatever can it be?
It's for a celebration.
Come, open it with me!

Rabbit Joe Has a Party

7 Read *Rabbit Joe Has a Party.* What does Rabbit Joe have? Write. Choose words from the box.

cake
carrots
hamburgers
ice cream
lettuce
pizza

He has carrots. He doesn't have hamburgers.

_____

_____

8 Do you like the story? Draw a face.

   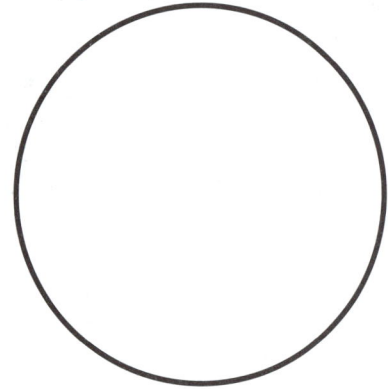

9 **What do you want at your party?**
Draw and color. Write.

Review

10 **Listen and read. Match. Draw a line.**

1. I have rice.

2. I have cake.

3. I have milk.

4. I have a sandwich.

5. I have a present.

6. I have ice cream.

Cut-out Activity ✂----------------

A. What are your favorite foods?
   Draw and write.

B. Cut. Show and say.

Students draw and color four favorite foods. Use the squares to build a horizontal bar graph on the classroom wall, with labels of each type of food on the left side of the graph and horizontal rows of squares to the right of their corresponding labels.

Unit 7

69

Play Time

1 **Listen and color. Cut and glue. Say.**

The Toy Box

I have a toy box, big and brown.
I look inside and find a clown.
I have a toy box with twelve toys,
    some toys for girls,
    some toys for boys.

Clap your hands!
Clap your hands!
I play all day with my toy box.

I have a toy box. I look inside.
I see it's empty—now I can hide!

(Chorus)

Look. Write. Use words from the box.

in
on
under

1. The doll is _____ the table.

2. The car is _____ the box.

3. The box is _____ the table.

 TRACK 38 **Listen and read. Draw.**

Draw eleven balls under the table.
Draw twelve blocks on the table.
Draw thirteen crayons in the box.

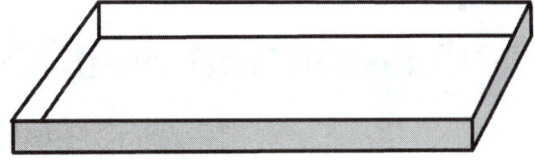

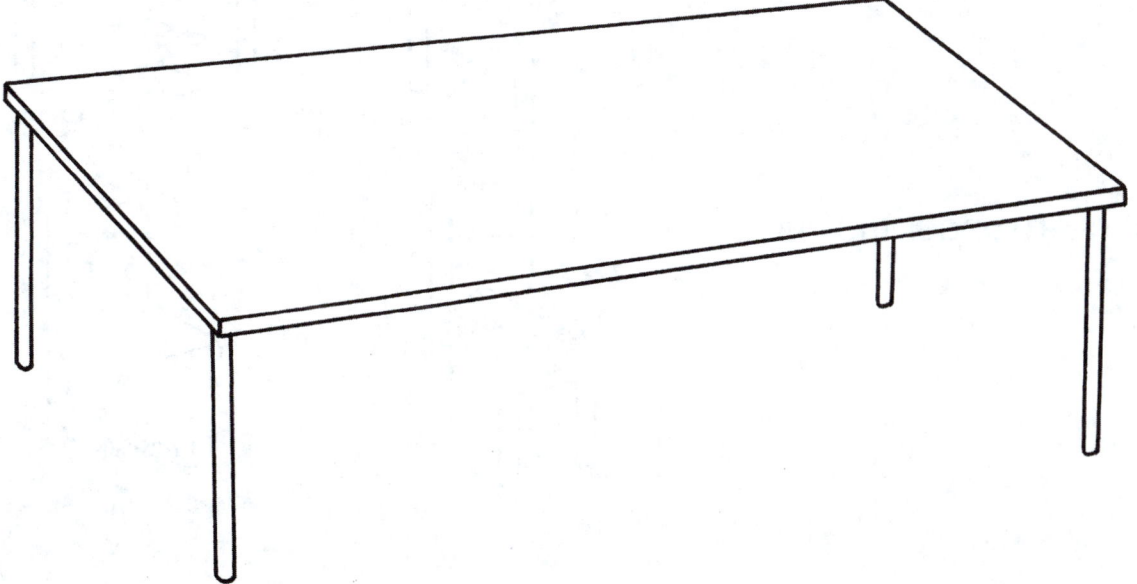

4 **Read and look. Write. Use words from the box.**

| doll | plane | yo-yo |

1. I want a _____.

2. I want a _____.

3. I want a _____.

5 **Listen and read. Circle.**

1. The kite is on the table.

2. The cars are under the chair.

 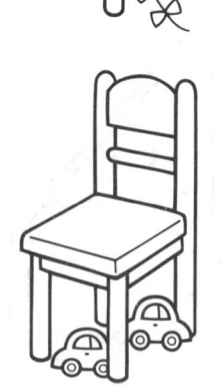

Listen. Write. Use words from the box.

Where Is the Boat?

bike
block
boat

Where is the _____?

The _____ is on the block.

The _____ is on the block.

Where is the _____?

The _____ is on the bike.

The _____ is on the bike.

Where is the _____?

The _____ is rolling away!

Oh, no! Oh, no! Oh, no!

7 **What is it? Draw a line from A to B to C. Finish with Z.**

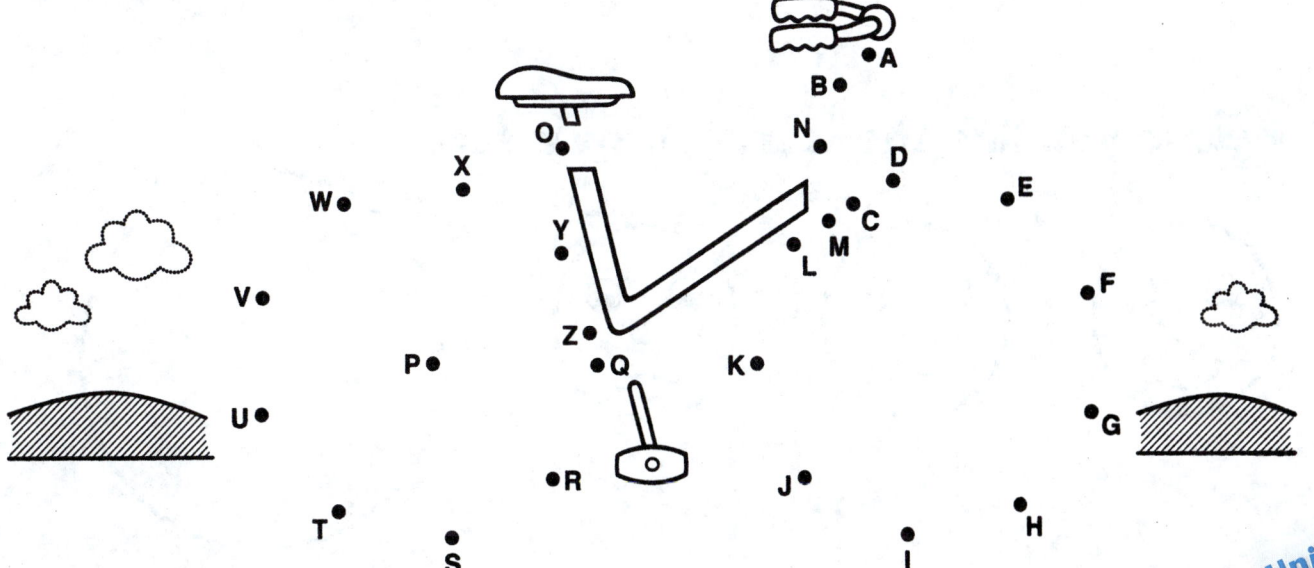

Where's My Bear?

8 Read *Where's My Bear?*
Listen and read. Circle.

I. What does the boy want?

2. Where do they look?

 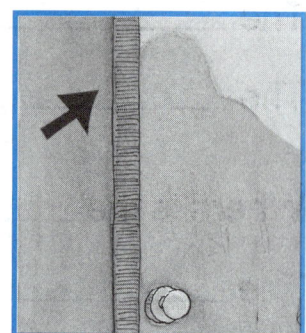

3. Who finds it?

4. Who has the teddy bear?

9 Do you like the story? Draw a face.

   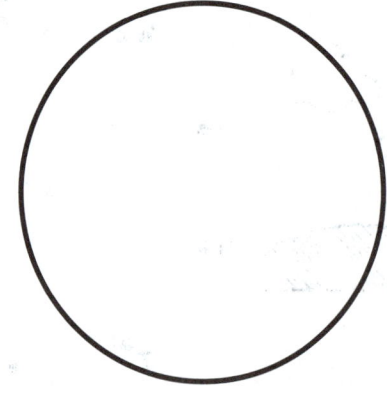

10 **Change the story. Where is the teddy bear?**
Draw and color. Write. Say.

The teddy bear is _____.

Review

11 **Look. Read and write.**

in	on	under

1. The cars are _____ the toy box.

2. The skates are _____ the chair.

3. The bear is _____ the desk.

ball	bike	dolls
kite	planes	yo-yo

4. The _____ are on the bed.

5. The _____ is under the table.

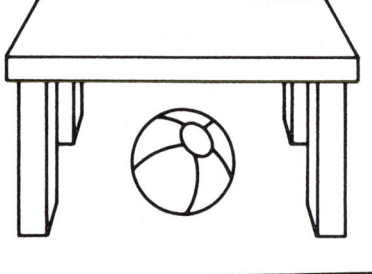

6. The _____ is in the box.

Cut-out Activity ✂-------------------------------

A. Find a partner.
B. Cut. Make words and say.

a	k	e
r	i	c
o	d	f
n	t	j

Students combine the alphabet cards to form words. (Students can use one set or combine two sets.) Words will vary, but may include the following: *marker, paper, four, two, green, pink, red, father, parents, hair, toes, dress, jacket, bed, cooking, reading, duck, worm, cake, rice, bear, bike, boat, car, skates, train.*

b	a	w
i	p	e
u	h	s
m	n	g

At the Playground

1 Listen. Cut. Match and glue.

Having Fun

We're kicking a ball.	We're having a snack.	We're singing a song.
We're dancing around.	We're stopping to talk.	We're flying a kite.

Read and color.

This bike is purple.
That bike is blue.

These books are pink.
Those books are red.

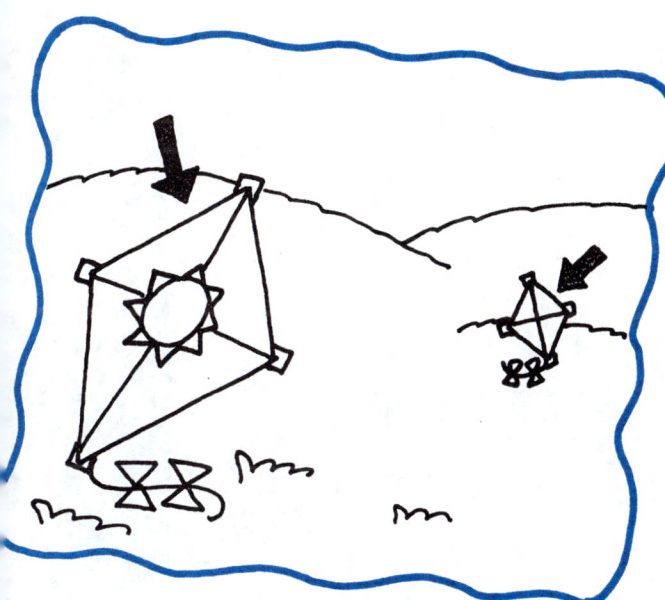

This kite is orange.
That kite is green.

These balls are brown.
Those balls are yellow.

What are you doing? Draw and color. Write.

eating	kicking	playing a game
riding	skating	throwing

_____

4 **Listen and match. Draw a line.**

Kicking, Singing, Skating

He's kicking.
He's kicking.
He's kicking a ball.

She's singing.
She's singing.
She's singing a song.

He's skating.
He's skating.
Watch out. Don't fall!

5 **Find the words. Circle.**

T	G	B	I	K	L	P
S	K	A	T	I	N	G
I	Y	L	U	C	I	O
N	F	L	T	K	R	E
G	D	G	H	I	Q	W
I	S	S	O	N	G	A
N	J	K	L	G	M	B
G	R	P	Z	C	V	N

ball
kicking
singing
skating
song

Unit 9

85

Tony Is Reading

 **6** **Read *Tony Is Reading*.**
What is Tony doing? Listen and circle.

1.

yes   no

2.

yes   no

3.

yes   no

4.

yes   no

 7 **Do you like the story? Draw a face.**

   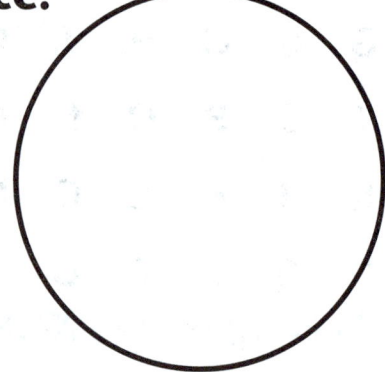

8 What happens next? What does Tony do?
Draw and color. Write.

_____.

Review

9 **Listen. Read and circle.**

1. No, he isn't.
   Yes, he is.

2. No, he isn't.
   Yes, he is.

3. No, she isn't.
   Yes, she is.

4. No, she isn't.
   Yes, she is.

10 **Look. Read and circle. Color.**

This / **That** kite is purple.

These / **Those** books are brown.

Cut-out Activity ✂ ------------------------------

A. Find a partner.
B. Cut and sort. Show and say.

pencil	bedroom	father
horse	hand	pizza
pants	doll	desk
sister	ears	jacket

Partners sort their word cards into the following categories: *school, family, parts of the body, clothing, rooms in a house, animals, food,* and *toys.* They can do this on their desks or glue the words on paper. Encourage students to think of more words to add.

bird	book	kitchen
eyes	rice	grandmother
bathroom	shirt	ball
skates	hot dog	cow

1 Color and say the letters.

Aa Bb Cc Dd
Ee Ff Gg Hh

2 Look at the picture. Write the letter. Say the word.

j_a_cket

__lephant

__anana

__at

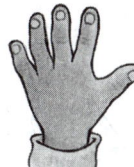

__and

__ame

__ar

__oll

__pple

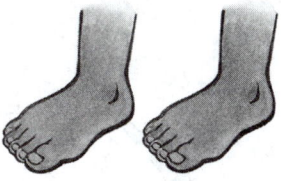

__eet

Color and say the letters.

Ii Jj Kk Ll Mm
Nn Oo Pp Qq

 **Look at the picture. Write the letter. Say the word.**

bedroo__   __ump rope   __ce cream

__range   __arker   __ion

__encil   __ose   __ing   __ueen

1 **Color and say the letters.**

Rr Ss Tt Uu Vv
Ww Xx Yy Zz

2 **Look at the picture. Write the letter. Say the word.**

__indow

__iolin

__andwich

__ellow

__mbrella

fo__

__en

__obot

__ebra

ha__

1 **Say the words. How many times do you hear *p* as in *pen*?**

pants   paper   party   pen   pencil   picnic   puppet   purple

2 **Do the crossword puzzle. Write words with *p* as in *pen*.**

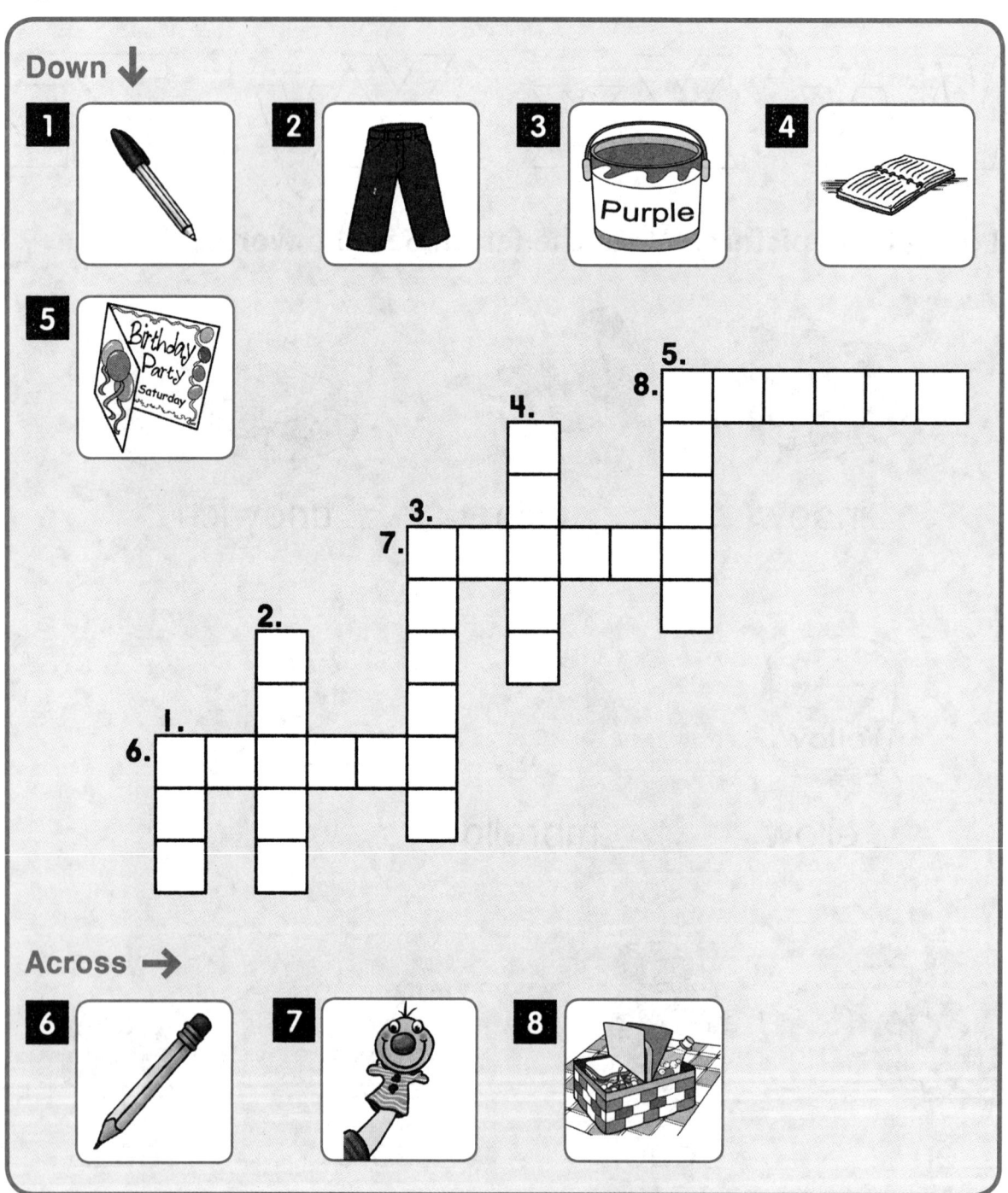

Down ↓

1 2 3 Purple 4

5 Birthday Party Saturday

5.
8.
4.
3.
7.
2.
1.
6.

Across →

6 7 8

1 Say the words. How many times do you hear *e* as in *bed*?

bed   desk   egg   leg   pen   pencil   red   seven

2 Penny wants eggs. Find the path using words with *e* as in *bed*.

Start

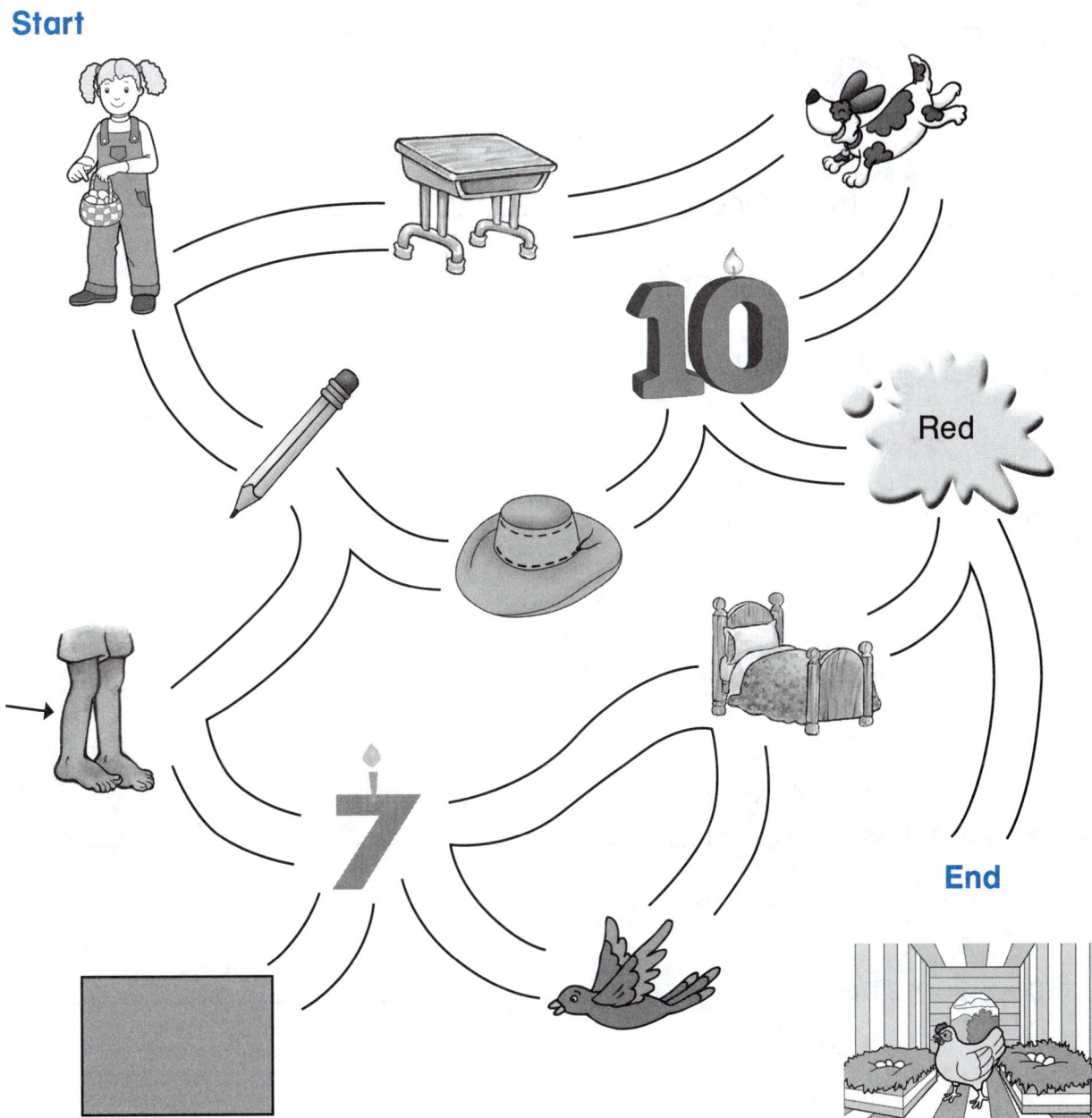

Red

End

1 Say the words. How many times do you hear *r* as in *red*?

ear   rabbit   rake   rectangle   robot   room   run   worm

2 Look at the picture and write a complete sentence. Say the sentence.

1. The ___ is running. _____

2. The ___ is walking. _____

3. The ___ is eating. _____

4. That ___ is crawling. _____

5. My sister is in her ___ . _____

6. My brother likes ___ . _____

7. Rosa wants her ___ . _____

8. My favorite color is ___ . _____

Red

1 Say the words. How many times do you hear **b** as in **ball**?

ball   balloon   banana   baby   bird   book   bus   robot

2 Color the rainbow. Look at the pictures. Write the words at the end of the rainbow.

balloon _____

_____ _____

_____ _____

1 Say the words. How many times do you hear **a** as in *bat*?

ant   apple   backpack   bath   family   hat   jacket   Saturday

2 Draw an X over the word that doesn't have the same sound as the **a** in *bat*.

1.

2.

3.

4.

3 Look at 2. Write the words that have the same sound as the **a** in *cat*.

____rabbit_____   _____   _____   _____

_____   _____   _____   _____

1 Say the words. How many times do you hear *s* as in *sock*?

hats   pants   salad   sandwich   seven   sister   socks   song

2 Do the crossword puzzle. Write words with *s* as in *sock*.

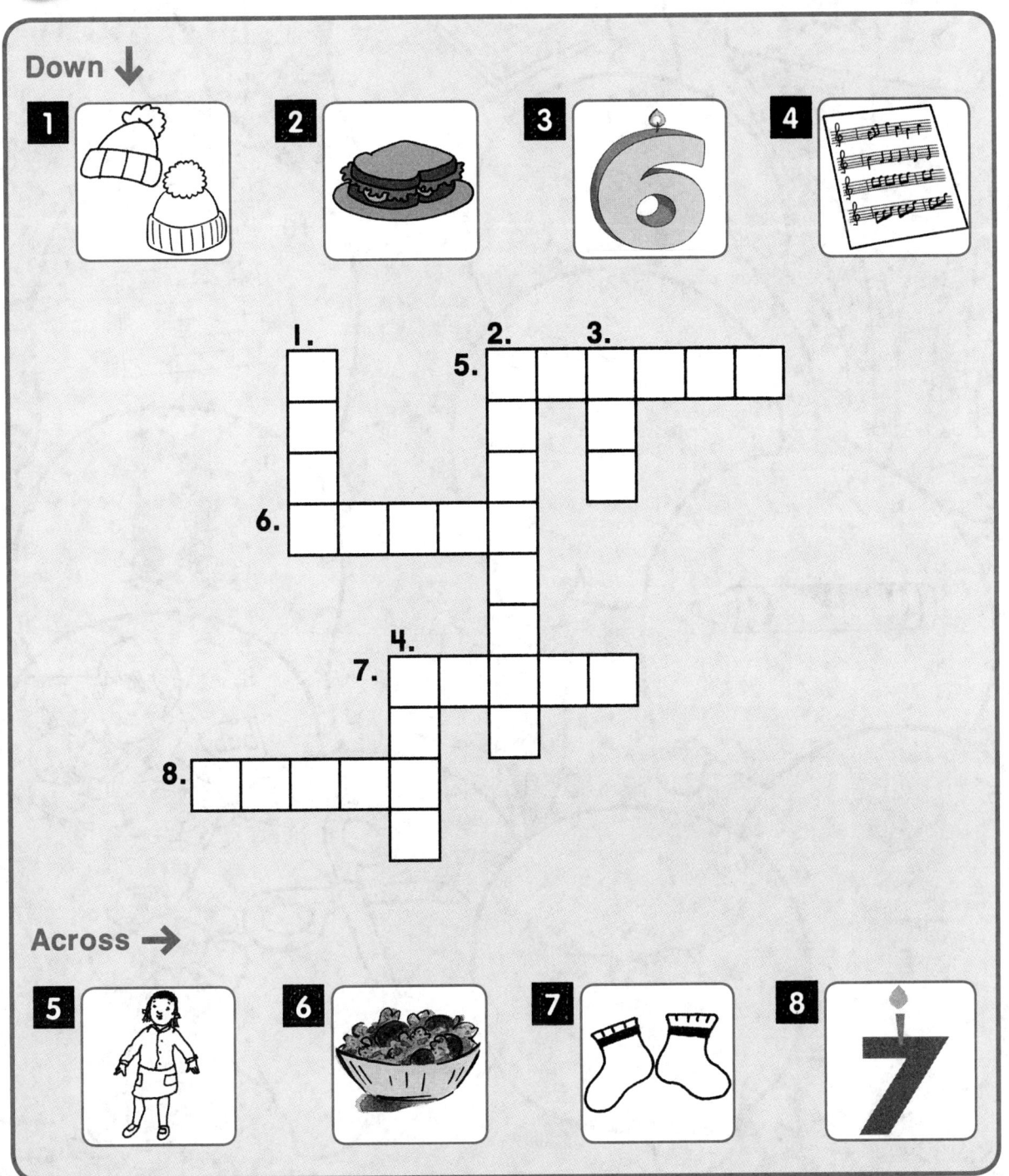

Down ↓

Across →

Move your game piece. Point and say.

Move your game piece. Point and say.

Move your game piece. Point and say.

Review board game, units 7–9

Subject Pronouns: Write.

| he | I | it | she | they | we | you | you |

_____ _____ _____ _____

_____ _____ _____ _____

 The Verb *Be*: Write.

| am | are | are | are |
| are | is | is | is |

I _____   we _____

you_____   you _____

he _____   they _____

she_____

it _____

3 **The Verb _Be_:** Write _am, are,_ or _is._

Hi! I _____ Gloria. And this _____

my friend Ana. We _____ six years old.

How old _____ you?

4 **The Verb _Have_:** Write.

has	has	has	have	have	have	have	have

I _____   we _____

you _____   you _____

he _____   they _____

she _____

it _____

5 **The Verb _Have_:** Write _has_ or _have._

Look! I _____ a frog.

Look! It _____ three arms.

Look! We _____ black hair.

6 **Present Progressive of *Wear*:** Write.

I _____ shorts.

You _____ shorts.

He _____ shorts.

She _____ shorts.

We _____ shorts.

They _____ shorts.

7 **Present Progressive:** Write.

| dance | jump | ride | run |

1. He _____ a bike.

2. Look! I _____ rope.

3. Look! I _____.

4. She _____.

8 **Questions:** Write.

1. _____ you five years old?   No, I'm six.

2. _____ does she have?   She has pizza.

3. _____ is the book?   It's on the table.